WITHDRAWN

Epic God-Talk

"The Apocalypse: St. John Devours the Book." Woodcut by
Albrecht Dürer. National Gallery of Art, Washington, D.C.

EPIC GOD-TALK

Paradise Lost and the Grammar of Religious Language

by
THOMAS MERRILL

McFarland & Company, Inc., Publishers
Jefferson, North Carolina, and London

Library of Congress Cataloguing-in-Publication Data

Merrill, Thomas F.
  Epic God-talk.

  Bibliography: p.
  Includes index.
  1. Milton, John, 1608–1674. Paradise lost. 2. God
in literature. 3. Theology in literature. 4. Christian
poetry, English — History and criticism. 5. Epic poetry,
English — History and criticism. I. Title.
  PR3562.M47 1986   821'.4   85-29385

ISBN 0-89950-194-X (acid-free natural paper)

Printed in the United States of America.

McFarland   Box 611   Jefferson NC 28640

To Mary

Contents

1

Introduction

"To a Christian, unfortunately, both art and science are secular activities, that is to say, small beer."
— W.H. Auden[1]

"God-talk," as John Macquarrie defines it, "is a form of discourse professing to speak about God." It is "rather a strange kind of language," he adds, that "seems to be different from our everyday discoursing about what is going on in the world."[2] It is different, most analysts of religious language would claim, because it is semantically oriented to God rather than the natural world. As David Crystal and Derek Davy point out, "Regardless of the purpose of the piece of religious language being examined — whether it be a statement of belief, or a prayer of praise or supplication — it is the case that the meaning of the whole derives from, and can be determined only by reference to this concept of 'God.'"[3] On these grounds and others, it has become fashionable to speak of religious discourse — God-talk — as a language whose logical conduct is uniquely different from that of so-called ordinary language even down to its very grammar.

The elevation of God-talk to special logical status in the last few decades has exposed it to systematic attention for the first time and has analytically confirmed what, as we shall see, seventeenth-century preachers so fervently declared from the pulpit, that such language is not only semantically eccentric but aggressively performative — it *does* what it says.

In a larger cultural sense, however, our recent acknowledgment of God-talk's special logical status is striking linguistic confirmation of Mircea Eliade's bleak observation that "the *completely* profane world, the wholly desacralized cosmos, is a recent discovery in the history of the

1

human experience."[4] "God is dead," said Nietzsche, and it would now appear that even the *word* "God," if not dead, is at least in a state of quarantine. Such a quarantine of God-talk from ordinary language perhaps would not have completely baffled John Milton, aware as he was of the fine distinctions between the natural and rectified reasons, but he surely would have been saddened by the linguistic poverty that the absence of their interaction assured, for any set of linguistic circumstances which divorces the functions of the sacred and the profane, that is, logically segregates the ordinary language of the world from "God," or God-talk from the ordinary language of the world, guarantees a universe of discourse far too diminished to contain the sweep of a Christian enterprise like *Paradise Lost*.

"What I want," said T.S. Eliot, "is a literature which should be *un-consciously*, rather than deliberately and defiantly, Christian."[5] What his words seem to lament is a time when "God" was not such a logical intruder into everyday language, as seems the case today, but a lexical constituent in good standing — a time considerably prior to the 1935 publication of *Language, Truth and Logic,* in which A.J.A. Ayer could seriously contend that "the theist, like any moralist, may believe that his experiences are cognitive experiences, but, unless he can formulate his 'knowledge' in propositions that are empirically verifiable, we may be sure that he is deceiving himself."[6] In Ayer's words "empirically verifiable" we hear the first symptoms of linguistic desacralization. He becomes the spokesman for a linguistic empiricism that demands to see the Emperor's clothes, that assumes that all philosophical inquiry is merely the consequence of muddled language, and proposes that a "purification" of the language of its "non-sense" (propositions which cannot be empirically verified or reduced to tautology) would automatically dispel the confused concerns that have traditionally occupied the attentions of philosophers and, presumably, theologians.

Imagine Milton attempting to "justify the ways of God to men" in such a desacralized linguistic climate. Imagine further a contemporary literary critic, having unconsciously assimilated the faintest residue of such reductionist views, presuming that he is equipped to illuminate for us all that is going on in *Paradise Lost*. If these seem remote concerns, consider this not untypical admonishment by a recent critic that we be "serious readers" of *Paradise Lost*. "All I mean by 'reading seriously' is that we try to believe what he [Milton] says," the critic explains. "We attend to what the words mean because we want to understand what Milton means. But it is just by attending to what the words mean in their full and normal senses that we are thrown into confusion."[7] The implications of that last sentence, and particularly the phrase "full and normal senses," smack sufficiently of the linguistic reductionism of logical positivism to alert us that such a "serious reading" is unlikely to evoke anything close to the Christian epic that Milton wrote.

Theologians, of course, have worried about linguistic reductionism for some time. Jean Ladrière voices a common lament of modern theists when he complains that our contemporary "enterprise of neo-positivism . . . appears as a vast programme of transcribing all forms of language into the privileged language of science" and that "the form of mind generated by the scientific praxis is hardly compatible with the type of attitude implied by faith."[8] Here is a theologian fearful of the scientification of the very vehicle which nourishes his faith, but even among theologians and philosophers who consider the threat of positivism to have crested, there lingers the concern that its influence subtly persists in our linguistic habits. The late Carl Michalson, for example, warned his theological colleagues of the "ghost of logical positivism"[9] that he detected lurking, though renounced, in their analytical machinery. Is it time for a similar examination of the analytical machinery of literary criticism, particularly when it is applied to genuinely religious texts? If an *assimilated* as opposed to a segregated God-talk (one that is, as Eliot recommends, not defiantly deliberate but unconscious) enriches the religious conduct of *Paradise Lost*, is there any way that we, suffering from varying degrees of contemporary desacralization, can render ourselves alive to its sacred promptings, or has the "ghost of logical positivism" so chilled our sensitivity (and hence our awareness) to the *religious* activity of the poem that we are terminally numb to its function as a holy thing?

This book proposes that some of the numbness can be quickened through a simple study of how God-talk in fact communicates, and how it communicates specifically in our greatest English Christian epic.

In his famous essay "Gods,"[10] John Wisdom included a parable that has since become a classic because of the rich articulation possibilities it lends to the modern controversy surrounding religious language. The parable was parodied by Antony Flew, whose version I present here because it happens to point up a number of other matters that bear on the God-talk of *Paradise Lost:*

> Once upon a time two explorers came upon a clearing in the jungle. In the clearing were growing many flowers and many weeds. One explorer says, 'Some gardener must tend this plot.' The other disagrees, 'There is no gardener.' So they pitch their tents and set a watch. No gardener is seen. So they set up a barbed-wire fence. They electrify it. They patrol with blood-hounds. (For they remember that H.G. Wells' *The Invisible Man* could both be smelt and touched though he could not be seen) but no shrieks suggest that some intruder has received a

shock. No movements of the wire ever betray an invisible climber. The bloodhounds never give a cry. Yet still the Believer is not convinced. 'But there is a gardener, invisible, intangible, insensible to electric shocks, a gardener who has no scent and makes no sound, a gardener who comes secretly to look after the garden which he loves.' At last the Sceptic despairs, 'But what remains of your original assertion? Just how does what you call an invisible, intangible, eternally elusive gardener differ from an imaginary gardener or even from no gardener at all?'[11]

Like all good parables, this one is open-ended and "teases the mind into active thought."[12] Flew sees it as an irrefutable demonstration of the "unfalsifiability" of religious propositions, that is, their refusal to permit any evidence to count against them. As he colorfully puts it, the parable shows how a "fine brash hypothesis" is "killed by inches, the death of a thousand qualifications."[13] Professor Wisdom, on the other hand, views it as a defense of religious logic. It demonstrates to him how "it is possible to have before one's eyes all the items of a pattern and still to miss the pattern."[14] Wisdom's Believer is not a debator on the run, a religious apologist whose faith-sponsored "evidence" suffers slow attrition before the pressure of sense-sponsored facts, but one who sees a pattern that his friend cannot.

Does the parable have anything to say about the modern appreciation of *Paradise Lost?* My hope is that it may tease us into active thought about how literary explorers in today's "desacralized" jungle might assess the flowers and weeds they discover in the garden of Milton's epic. Wisdom would ask them to consider that what distinguished the responses of his sceptic and believer to the identical evidence in front of them was not intelligence, nor taste, nor imagination, nor special information available to one and not the other, but that one simply saw a pattern that the other did not, a pattern generated by an "invisible gardener" who was not functionally present in the garden the other saw. Is there a danger that today's readers of *Paradise Lost* may be blind to the pattern generated by the "invisible gardener" that presides over Milton's poem? Let us be sure we understand Wisdom's point. He is *not* talking about the kind of critical relativism popular today which arbitrarily takes a "religious point of view" toward any and all literary works, sacred and profane. The pattern his Believer sees is no subjective illusion. It exists. The issue is whether or not today's readers possess the linguistic proficiency to detect it.

For must of us today, the God of *Paradise Lost* is virtually a corpse awaiting critical autopsy (having long ago met the "death by a thousand qualifications") and the poem which that corpse inhabits, a "noble monument to dead ideas."[15] True, we probably value *Paradise Lost* highly as "a work of art," a stylistic masterpiece, a grand design and an imaginative literary marvel, but perhaps because we cannot value it *as truth*, we expose our Achilles' heel, for in separating the dancer from the dance, that is, the poem's artistic form from its religious vocation, we tacitly acknowledge another separation of even greater consequence — the linguistic separation of the sacred and the profane. By capitulating to this separation we acquiesce to semantic idolatry.

By semantic idolatry I mean the hermeneutical abuse that occurs when the *means to* revelation is taken for the revelation itself. It is a natural consequence of "desacralization" which causes particular mischief when it afflicts critical interpretations of noncontemporary Christian texts like *Paradise Lost*, for not only is there the problem of sorting out differences of historical and cultural bias that separate the seventeenth and twentieth centuries, but the more subtle, yet deeply rooted, differences of ontological commitment that distinguish the sacred from secular language. Today our interest in *Paradise Lost* understandably centers on its achievement as a "work of art," but in judging it exclusively as a "work of art" do we not forfeit the experience of it as a "holy thing" and consign ourselves to the pointlessness of rendering a *non*religious account of an essentially religious activity?

An extreme example of what I have in mind is A.J.A. Waldock's reading of Book Nine of *Paradise Lost* in which Adam must choose between sharing Eve's fate or maintaining his obedience to God. I apologize for citing such a vulnerable instance of "anti-Miltonic" criticism, but the bluntness of Waldock's "literary" bias makes the distinction I want to expose more clearcut than more subtle versions at this point could. Waldock contends that Milton erred in depicting this episode by presenting us with "an unbearable collision of values." We are asked to set aside "one of the highest, and really one of the oldest, of all human values: self-lessness in love . . .[for] the mere doctrine that God must be obeyed." He even insinuates that Milton himself, although "not in a position to admit it," felt that Adam was doing a "worthy thing" by eating the apple and joining Eve in sin. The resultant conflict, as Waldock sees it, is that "the poem asks from us, at one and the same time, two incompatible responses. It requires us, not tentatively, not half-heartedly (for there can be no place really for half-heartedness here) but with the full weight of our minds to believe that he did wrong."[16]

Waldock's brief against Milton is that he permits a collision of ethical and divine values and that the incompatibility of these values as they converge on Adam "is so critical" that it pulls the reader "in two ways" and cheats him of the "full-hearted response that a great tragic theme allows and compels."

The demands of tragedy and the demands of faith *do* pull in two ways in the scene, but the question is whether this alleged literary "error" may not in fact be a calculated religious success. Waldock's error is in failing to read a religious situation religiously. What Milton intended as an occasion for the evocation of religious discernment, Waldock takes for a "typical tragic conflict." Because Milton condones the "unbearable collision of these contentious claims, Waldock finds him a casuistic blunderer and a dramatic tyro. Never once does he consider that the "unbearable collision of values" here and elsewhere in *Paradise Lost* is deliberate, or that he may have idolatrously fixed his attention on a model, missing the religious disclosure that model was intended to evoke. For Waldock, it would seem, Milton's models are opaque.

Very well, how do we recapture Milton's religious intention with the scene? How do we read it as God-talk? A clue might be William Perkins' seventeenth-century counsel concerning the particular case of conscience when "God commaunds one thing & the magistrate commaundes the flat contrarie; in this case . . . the latter must give place to the former, and the former alone in this case must be obeyed: Act. 4.19 *Whether it be right in the sight of God to obey you rather than God, judge ye.*"[17]

With the epic before us we do not need Perkins to tell us that "love and honor to God must be valued, painful as it seems, above love and honor to one's wife," because Milton forces us to share this "unbearable collision of values" along with Adam. Of course "we are pulled in two ways" as we read the episode; Milton intended for us to be. Adam's dilemma forces us, perhaps as we cannot force ourselves, to experience the claim of sacred obligation, to work through to the awareness that it is the "more worthy" thing that Adam love and obey God than that he covet, however gallantly, Eve. To be sure, we may feel with Waldock that a morally reprehensible duty is required of Adam, but that is the point. This is not a "typical tragic conflict" but a characteristically religious situation. The discernment engineered by Milton here precisely parallels the story of Abraham and Isaac: that the love of God must be set above all other loves — even those of wife or son.

Waldock sees in *Paradise Lost* exactly what Wisdom's sceptic sees in the jungle garden, but the issue is not, as it may appear on the face of it, a simple case of sacred and profane sensibilities looking at identical evidence and drawing different conclusions. There are patterns, and Wisdom suggests that

> wrongheadedness or wrongheartedness in a situation, blind-
> ness to what is there or seeing what is not, does not arise merely
> from mismanagement of language but is more due to connec-
> tions which are not mishandled in language, for the reason that
> they are not put into language at all.[18]

The "missing connections" in language are the primary justification for historical criticism. Wisdom's concern, however, is not the historical but the religious "replacement" of connections, and he may have had in mind when he speaks of "unspoken connections," the "gaps," "lacunae," and "mysterious omissions" which, according to Erich Auerbach, characterize the style of the Bible.[19] Such missing connections, Wisdom observes, are often "operative but not presented in language," and it is obvious that here is a prime source of interpretive blunder, particularly in cases where a relatively secular culture assays to understand the sacred literature of an older religious one, ignorant of its unspoken connections.

In some instances the unspoken connections implicit in religious discourse leave manifest signs of their presence. The "lacunae" or "paratactic gaps" that Auerbach detects even in the surface texture of biblical style witness a deficiency of connectives. In the Bible, for example, we find statements like "God said, Let there be light; and there was light"; "Once I was blind. Now I see." The gaps in the middle of these assertions are repositories of religious faith, experience, dogma and mystery which are the "unspoken connectives" which the sacred ethos of a particular age unconsciously supplies.

We will be savoring other symptoms of unspoken connections which characterize religious language such as the "logical improprieties" spawned by the sheer presence of the word "God" in an otherwise secular context or how profane models are theologically qualified in logically scandalous ways. Most of all, we will be immersing ourselves in the general performative, as opposed to indicative, manner in which religious utterances characteristically behave. More often than not, they *do* rather than describe, and this pervasively dynamic logical style is what gives genuine religious language its distinctive cachet.

In case the concept of a performative language strikes some as an inappropriate intrusion of a modern analytical concept upon a seventeenth-century Christian epic (not to mention a rather presumptuous notion to include in Milton's store of creative talents), we may recall that it was still commonplace in Milton's time to speak unselfconsciously of the "operation" of the Word of God upon hearers. Thomas Cartwright, for example, could casually point out that preaching "is the excellentest and most *ordinary* means to work faith by in the hearts of the hearers . . . The *ordinary* ways whereby God regenerateth his children is by the Word of God which is preached."[20] William Perkins, author of the most famous and influential manual on "puritan" preaching, *The Arte of Prophecying* (1609), remarks that the "excellency of the Word" is equally concerned with its "operation" as with its "nature," pointing out that "the operation . . . converteth men, and though it be flatly contrary to the reason and affections of men, yet it winneth them into itselfe."[21]

Perkins also contended that "Absolution is conferred, or withheld in preaching,"[22] and even John Donne commonly counseled his parishioners that "the Holy Ghost casts a net over the whole congregation, in this Ordinance of preaching, and catches all that break not out."[23] These random instances of a commonplace belief that language performs as well as informs relate, of course, to the *preached* Word of God, but they at least suggest that the seventeenth-century attitude toward language as an aggressively dynamic force was lively and perceptive. Perkins lists the operational functions of the Word as two: "to discern the spirit of man" and "to bind the conscience."[24] It would seem that these functions rather precisely parallel the claims of today's analysts when they speak of religious assertions as "self-involving" (Donald Evans), "*self*-consuming" (Stanley Fish) or words that precipitate "discernment-commitment situations" (Ian Ramsey). The idea of language doing what it says would not have struck the seventeenth-century preaching theorist or church-goer as unusual in the least. Indeed, he would need little tutoring to grasp the essentials of modern hermeneutics, for it was already a fundamental part of his spiritual experience.

Paradise Lost is not a sermon, but in a sense it shares some of the sermon's vocational thrust as well as the peculiarly religious logic of its language. If John Milton had followed his own resolutions and the intentions of his parents and friends, his justification of the "ways of God to men" (I, 26) would have probably issued from the pulpit rather than the pen. His training at Cambridge was for the priesthood, and only his conscientious refusal to "straight perjure or split his faith" by taking the oath of orders that Laud's prelatical "tyranny" required kept him from a destined evangelical career. And so, we recall, he was "church-outed,"[25] but certainly not "outed" from his commitment to a Christian vocation. He refused to forfeit, for example, his "clergy-right whereto," he insisted, "Christ hath entitled him."[26] Laymen, he claimed, were a "royal priest-hood" who had pastoral obligations of equal status to those who were officially ordained. He was particularly concerned to establish that poetic abilities were not only "the inspired gift of God" but were "of power beside the office of a pulpit."[27]

This book hardly urges a program of evangelism for readers of *Paradise Lost*. It does not insist that all readers and critics of *Paradise Lost* be born (or "born again") Christians. It does propose, however, that the application of recent techniques for analyzing the dynamics of religious language can effectly help us to restore the "unspoken connections" implicit in *Paradise Lost* and thus provide some remedy for the secular aloofness which I am convinced stands between the aesthetic *Paradise Lost* we read today and the religious enterprise Milton originally conducted.

2

Words About God

"Primo grammatica videamus, verum ea theo-logica."

— Martin Luther[1]

Whatever we decide to call *Paradise Lost* — an inspired prophecy, a superior form of political science, a sacral document, a virtual myth, a device for reader entrapment — it is at its most fundamental level simply "words about God." I borrow this deceptively banal phrase from Kenneth Burke to emphasize that my concern with the epic is "not directly with religion, but rather with the *terminology* of religion; not directly with man's relationship to God, but rather with his relationship with the *word* 'God.' "[2] I want to assess the extent to which "God" (and the eccentric logical style that it generates) seizes control of the poem's semantic terrain as it deploys to meet the manifold challenge of expressing the inexpressible.

Words About God[4] is also the title of an anthology of essays on religious language edited by the late Bishop of Durham, Ian Ramsey, and I hope that this additional allusion might further locate the quarter from which I will approach *Paradise Lost:* not along routes already familiar to literary exploration (myth, accommodated language, typology, prophecy, hierophany) but from amidst the conversation of theologians and philosophers of religion who in recent decades, reacting to logical positivism's charge that words about God amount to nonsense, have concurred with Burke's premise that "whether or not there is a realm of the 'supernatural,' there are *words* for it"[4] and have taken up the investigation of *how* such words are in fact used in their typical settings: public and private devotion, preaching, systematic theology, the Bible and, I would add, distinctly Christian literary expressions such as *Paradise Lost.*

By "distinctly Christian expression" I do not mean literature incidentally *about* Christian material, even though it may exploit Christian tropes and diction; I mean literature whose language is *of* the Christian experience — Christian through and through down to its grammatical and ontological roots. My claim is that the words about God which make up *Paradise Lost* (like those of God-talk generally) place special logical pressures on otherwise independent literary decisions, pressures which Milton unconsciously felt but which dictated (more than we might expect) the narrative and linguistic conduct of his poem.

Friedrich Waismann likes to use the term "language strata" to describe the difference in *logical style* one feels when one "compares such statements as: a material object statement, a sense-datum statement, a law of nature, a geometric proposition, a statement describing a dream, a proverb, and so forth."[5] To Waismann's list I would want to add "a God statement," for whether we term these differences in logical style "language strata," "language games" (Wittgenstein), "universes of discourse" (Urban), "discourse situations" (Macquarrie), "speech acts" (Austin and Searle), "speech events" (Ebeling) or "language habitats" (Donald Evans), the fact remains, as Wittgenstein eventually discovered, that meaning in language is determined not by rigid referential definition, semantic behavior of a particular stratum of language is invariably dictated by a commitment to a logical premise. "Change the logic," says Waismann, "and then the propositions will take on new meanings."[6]

The logical premise of God-talk (and the source of its eccentricity) is, of course, God, and god is linguistically mischievous because, as E.L. Mascall puts it, He "is by definition an infinite and suprasensible being, while all the language that we have in which to talk about him has been devised in order to describe and discuss the finite objects of our sense experience."[7] Mascall describes for us a situation in which God is curiously at war with the very medium through which He relates to man, and this kind of logical skirmish was precisely the kind of muddle that early linguistic empiricists like G.E. Moore, Bertrand Russell, the early Wittgenstein and the Vienna Circle hoped to expunge from logically valid propositions. Russell succinctly explains the grounds upon which the empiricists condemned the propositions of God-talk as "non-sense":

> A spoken sentence consists of a temporal series of events. A written sentence is a spatial series of bits of matter. Thus it is not surprising that language can represent the course of events in the physical world, preserving its structure in a more manageable form, and it can do this because it consists of physical events . . . if there were such a world as the mystic postulates, it would have a structure different from that of language, and would therefore be incapable of being verbally described.[8]

There is a tidy, scientific attractiveness to this explanation which gains its plausibility through a total indifference to any truth-authority other than the empirical evidence of the "physical world." Thus, Russell implicitly establishes scientific language as privileged, to the logical detriment of all other forms of expression. Like Waldock, who complained of the "unbearable collision of values" that Milton permitted in *Paradise Lost,* Russell and the linguistic empiricists complained of similarly unbearable collisions in the logic of not only God-talk, but all talk which refused to yield logically to the authority of the things and events of the "physical world," and their response was to initiate a purge.

That language's competency is limited to "the physical world" is a notion that would not have consciously occurred to John Milton nor his contemporaries, since their confidence in the reality of immaterial things had not yet been seriously challenged. Thus, their natural fluency in God-talk concealed from them the idiosyncracies of its use much in the same way that those having no second language generally fail to appreciate the logical pecularities of their native tongue. Linguistic empiricism, therefore, plays a positive role in the analysis of how God-talk functions, for it exposes logical eccentricities which otherwise would have remained buried in the familiarity of usage.

At any rate, analysis demonstrates that when "God" is dropped into the "privileged" language that Russell describes, it comes not only as an alien, non-physical anomaly, but as a rival ontological authority that competes with grammar itself for logical control. In this dynamic competition with grammar we find God-talk's essential uniqueness, for just as Russell describes a language that mirrors the "course of events in the physical world," so God-talk mirrors the course of events in *its* purview — the frontlines of ontological encounter where the claims of faith and the claims of the world engage in dynamic conflict. To put it another way, the word "God" embarrasses the language of the world, for it disturbs its complacency. It boldly asserts, according to Archbishop Temple's arithmetic, that "God minus the world equals God; whereas the world minus God equals nothing at all."[9]

God-talk does not take predication in the same way that ordinary proper nouns do. Compare, for example, the statements "God created the heavens and the earth" and "Christopher Wren created St. Paul's"; or "God is on my side" and "the police commissioner is on my side"; or yet again, "God loves me" and "Jenny loves me." Despite their apparent syntactical similarities, these comparisons are striking examples of logical asymmetry. If we replace "Christopher Wren," "the police commissioner," and "Jenny" with "God," we see at once the qualitative change that this oddly-behaved noun inflicts on the sentences. God's creativity means something rather more to the believer than Wren's. God's sustaining support is of a fundamentally different order than the backing of one's local police commissioner, and God's love suggests a comprehensiveness and quality hardly to be expected of anyone's Jenny. The sheer presence of "God," implicitly or explicitly felt within a linguistic context, radically alters the semantic landscape; it tyrannizes the structure of the discourse into which it is introduced. "God," quips I.M. Crombie, "is a very improper proper name."[10]

While we can only figuratively claim God-talk to be language independent in its own right (it boasts no unique formal properties aside from a few biblical archaisms and specialized theological vocabulary), we should not let that obscure the eccentricity of its logical and semantic conduct. God-talk is the language of the "physical world" placed under logical stress because it is *put to special use.* Some describe it as ordinary language that has been "stretched"[11] to include realities beyond the reach of conventional grammar.

"Stretched" also expresses how God-talk overextends its base to effect its characteristic double vision, for ideally, God-talk is a linguistic double exposure of sacred and profane truths. It simultaneously serves the rival logics of heaven and earth, and even though it never adequately reconciles them, the attempt itself, acknowledging as it does their competing ontological claims, assures it its distinctively kinetic double reference. This is the very essence of God-talk and the moment it is lost, either through authorial or interpretive failure, the blight of literalism sets in. Such literalism is fatal to the religious experience, for it stills the contentious ontological encounter that God-talk normally referees and reduces it to the mere "course of events in the physical world." Worse, literalism, by arresting and flattening God-talk's kinetic double vision, encourages the confusion of the *means* to revelation for the revelation itself — semantic idolatry.

"God," as we can see, is a jealously contentious word. It contests all rivals for linguistic control of any context in which it appears. Crystal and Davy, we recall, found God-talk's most distinctive feature to be how all its "lexical items can ultimately be referred . . . [to] the term 'God,' " adding that "this clear focal point is something which distinguishes religious language from other varieties."[12] Because it is the linguistic center of God-talk, "God" can be said to create its own vocabulary in that its semantic magnetism proselytizes otherwise independent denotations into its service. Not only biblically-sponsored words such as "cross," "altar," "crucifix" fall prey to its semantic pull, but virtually any word is subject to its transubstantiating power. "God" is not verbal magic — the God-talk it generates does not cause heathens automatically to fall on their knees when they hear it — but it does provoke logical dissonance by promoting an active conflict between the claims of faith and the claims of the world, and this causes interpretive problems for those who, like Waldock, unwittingly read its assertions as straightforward indicative statements.

"God" is improper referentially too. Ordinary proper nouns normally refer to persons, places, or things, or at least some reasonably conclusive concept, but when most people use the word "God," they refer to something that is anything but conclusive. Since God is ineffable, what people have in mind when they use the word "God" can at best be a *penultimate* referent, that is, a useful fiction composed of sanctioned figures standing in for what, in Gordon Kaufman's terms, is "some utterly unknowable X."[13] Kaufman labels this useful fiction the "available God,"[14] making the identical point Milton did in *The Christian Doctrine:* ". . . both in the literal and figurative descriptions of God, he is exhibited not as he really is, but in such a manner as may be within the scope of our comprehensions."[15]

That "God" refers to an "available" fiction rather than a real deity should alert us to the hazards of regarding God-talk as straightforwardly indicative. Rarely, in fact, is it informative. If it were, the very fictitiousness of "God's" available referent would guarantee the information to be false and, worse, idolatrous. True fluency in God-talk, therefore, requires that "God's" referent never be understood as an absolute but at best as a signpost which points, often inadequately, in the general direction one must explore in order to experience a sense of the real, ineffable God. To use a slogan popularized by General Semantics, "The map is not the territory,"[16] nor is God-talk the reality of God. Thus, one should never regard the utterances of God-talk as absolute conclusions, but rather, as Ian Ramsey once quaintly put it, "rules for significant stuttering."[17]

But God-talk's odd mode of reference involves more than the curious fictitiousness of the available God, for whereas the normal syntactical entailments of ordinary language are founded upon "horizontal" relationships of cause and sequence, God-talk disdains such coherence by disruptively intruding a "vertical" anomaly—God's will. This anomaly does not overpower the authority of the horizontal entailment; it merely destabilizes it. Thus, whatever coherence God-talk promises comes not from God nor from nature, but from the logical skirmish between them. Its effectiveness cannot be measured by inference, consistency or empirical verification but by the efficiency with which it transforms natural facts into religious disclosures. To state it with more technical precision, "The canons of formal logic do not apply *between* the utterances which are the protocol-statements of religion. The primary syntactical relationship for the language of living faith is that of equivalence, not entailment."[18]

When equivalence rather than entailment determines the

coherence of a literary enterprise, we discover that some of our conventional critical postulates lose their appropriateness. For example, the requirement that literature should exhibit an *internal* decorum — narrative consistency, coordination (rather than "collision" of values), uniformity of motivation, symmetry of structure, propriety of description, and so forth — could prove misleading in Christian works like *Paradise Lost* if it is later discovered that religious disclosure rather than literary decorum dictated their logic.

Even in terms of surface texture, as Erich Auerbach has argued, there is a discernible distinction between styles that are configured according to equivalence rather than entailment. In an entailed style like Homer's, for example,

> the separate elements of a phenomenon are most clearly placed in relation to one another; a large number of conjunctions, adverbs, particles, and other syntactical tools, all clearly circumscribed and delicately differentiated in meaning, delimit persons, things, and portions of incidents in respect to one another, and at the same time bring them together in a continuous and ever flexible connection; . . . a continuous rhythmic procession of phenomena passes by, and never is there a form left fragmentary or half-illuminated, never a lacuna, never a gap, never a glimpse of unplumbed depths.[19]

On the other hand, biblical style, which takes its structural authority from without, follows a decidedly different and equivalent pattern:

> . . . certain parts brought into high relief, others left obscure, abruptness, suggestive influence of the unexpressed, 'background' quality, multiplicity of meanings and the need for interpretation, universal historical claims . . . preoccupation with the problematic.[20]

In biblical language only selective points are made. There are deliberate, mysterious omissions which frustrate horizontally entailed interpretations:

> what lies between is non-existent; time and place are undefined and call for interpretation; thoughts and feelings remain unexpressed, are only suggested by silence and the fragmentary speeches; the whole, permeated with the most unrelieved suspense and directed towards a single goal . . . remains mysterious and fraught with background.[21]

Homer's epic world (very much like the linguistic world of Russell) is complete and self-contained; all that is necessary for its complete understanding is provided. It has a tightly caulked surface texture. All potential gaps and lacunae are bridged by syntactical ligature. It is a style that can be analyzed but not interpreted. Biblical style, on the other hand, not only invites, but demands, outside reference. Its paratactic gaps and open texture require interpretive filler which it assumes will be supplied by doctrine, creed and faith.

D.Z. Phillips once observed that "it is the status of the object addressed which determines the grammar of the talk,"[22] and the remarkable effect of the presence of the word "God" in a linguistic text certainly bears this out. Consider, for example, a verbal context containing the nouns "pasture," "water," "path," "valley," "table," "enemy," "oil," "house," and so forth. These, of course, are the determinative words of the Twenty-third Psalm and, as they are arranged in the Psalm, they make perfectly coherent worldly sense, so long as we ignore the initial controlling metaphor: "The *Lord* is my shepherd." "Lord," in its full theological sense as a surrogate for "God," stings the otherwise neutral passage into religious significance. The presence of the divine name in this psalm automatically "doubles" its dimensions without altering its constituents in any way.

Ian Ramsey casts some psychological light on how "God" accomplishes its improprieties when he suggests that " 'I' will never cease to be a useful guide for us when we are confronted by puzzles about 'God,' "[23] and so perhaps does Rudolph Bultmann when he declares that "the question of God and the question of myself are identical."[24] This is not to say that there is an actual equation between "God" and "I," or even a metaphorical relationship. The terms are structurally similar, however, in the sense that they are both bases for what Ramsey calls "significant tautologies" or "ultimates of explanation."[25] To illustrate his meaning he cites a fisherman's reply to the question: Why do you want to fish? " 'What a question. You know what fishing is for me. Fishing is fishing. Why did I want to fish? Because I'm I.' "[26] Such a tautology marks the point where empirical explanation reaches its limit and yields to a qualitatively different realm of inexpressible motives, and it parallels, Ramsey would argue, the qualitative transition that occurs when the language of the world psychologically transmutes into God-talk. Another "ultimate of explanation" might occur when in the throes of despair we sigh, "O God." It may come at the end of a long chain of subsidiary explanations for some deep-seated malaise: sorrow, fatigue, sickness, sense of sin, until finally we utter the ultimate explanation which attempts to express that which is beyond explanation, "O God." "O God" and "I'm I" are psychologically equivalent utterances and thus bear a logical relationship to each other. Both reveal a commitment of the entire personality. The lover loves his beloved because he is he and she is she.

When pressed for an explanation of his devotion to that particular woman and after exhausting the endless, yet somehow inconclusive subsidiary reasons (her flaming red hair, her pleasant disposition, her beautiful nose), he finally throws up his hands and replies, "Because that's the way I am. I am *I*, that's all."

The intimate parallelism of "I'm I" and "God" is explicit in the third chapter of Exodus. When God identifies Himself to Moses, He says simply: "I am that I am." We might have some insight into the divine linguistic strategy here if we consider that "I am that I am" is exactly the kind of "significant tautology" of which Ramsey speaks. As the evocation of a final explanation, "I am that I am" is a profound disclosure situation. It betrays its logical impropriety by operating less as a name than a riddle. The reason it does so is not only the Hebrew injunction against uttering the divine name, but because the riddle signals the exhaustion of all conceptual explanations of the Deity. The riddle appropriately honors God's mystery. Anything less than this ultimate explanation would literalize God, consigning the Creator to His own Creation where proper nouns take clearcut predication and mystery is anathema.

"I'm I" and "O God" are utterances that echo between the outer edges of two tangent language domains. Each is the "ultimate explanation" for its own domain and, as such, logically parallels the other. The difference, as we have seen, is that "I'm I" assimilates into the "course of events in the physical world," but when "God" is introduced into the world of a particular text, the text becomes alive with conflicting logical commitments which more often than not baffle the common sense. Adam knows the power of those conflicting commitments in Book Nine of *Paradise Lost* when, faced with the choice between Eve and God, he finds himself on the isthmus connecting "I'm I" and "God." Only such an "unbearable collision" of "significant tautologies" could possibly do justice to the ultimacy of Adam's decision. Considering the close logical kinship of these "ultimate explanations," we can perhaps understand Waldock's blunder in faulting Milton for "an unbearable collision of values" which, far from demonstrating the dramatic failure of that scene, gloriously illustrates the power of its genuinely evocative God-talk.

3
The Varieties of God-Talk

"What expresses *itself* in language, *we* cannot express by means of language."
— Wittgenstein[1]

If we claim that *Paradise Lost* and the Bible share a common logical style, by virtue of the performative presence of the word "God" active in both texts, it would be persuasive if we could compare excerpts from each and demonstrate their formal similarities. Unfortunately, it just does not work. The surface similarities are not convincingly there. Of course neither the style of the Bible nor *Paradise Lost* is monolithic; each employs a variety of stylistic forms in order to serve the propriety of its special purposes and circumstances. Prayers, for example, are formally distinct from parables, and invocations differ stylistically from narrative passages. But even roughly equivalent formal passages from the Bible and *Paradise Lost* generally fail to produce compelling stylistic similarities.

This is not from lack of trying. One of the most prominent trends in recent Milton scholarship has been the effort to establish the Bible rather than the Classics as *Paradise Lost's* stylistic fulcrum.[2] Genesis, Isaiah, Job, and Revelations have all been specifically cited as models, but almost as many studies have insisted upon the poem's non-biblical rationality. Dennis Burden, for instance, argues that *Paradise Lost* is a "logical" epic, an "exercise" in biblical "clarification, finding system and order in what could, if wrongly taken, appear to be random and inexplicable."[3] Stimulating as most studies of the relationship of *Paradise Lost* to the Bible are, none decisively stakes out a common linguistic ground between them that is convincingly clearcut.

The difficulty is that we tend to confuse logical style with formal style. Whatever direct indebtedness *Paradise Lost* owes to the Bible should not be expected to be formally prominent because its presence is embedded deeply in the logical structure of God-talk itself. The logical style is not something that Milton consciously imitated, but rather a style forced upon him by the inherent behavior of religious language itself, of which the Bible is the Christian norm. The German theologian Gerhard Ebeling exposes the subtle logical similarity between Scripture and Christian literature by pointing out that

> the Bible, with the incomparable power of its language, cannot and is not meant to be understood as a model for the language of faith, a pattern book of devout phraseology. The most appropriate use of the language of the Bible is when it enables us to produce our language of faith independently. . . . The Bible shows faith how to use its own words.[4]

Biblical God-talk and such specimens of the "independent" language of faith as *Paradise Lost* do not necessarily share a formal style, but they do operate within a common ontological context which lends them a correspondingly common logical distinctiveness. "A language can be marked throughout," says Ebeling, "by the understanding of reality which is dominant in it."[5] In showing faith how to use its words, the Bible presents a normative reality—a "logical habitat"[6]—within which the words of faith are to be understood. Thus, if we are convinced of the authenticity of the God-talk in *Paradise Lost*, we should be able to clear up most of the confusions the poem may present by relating them to a biblical rather than a natural logical setting.

It is important to understand that the biblical setting is not something that can be retrieved through historical research. Of course biblical historians can tell us what a word "probably meant at a particular period in a particular community; or what a word in a particular biblical passage probably meant to a particular man who wrote it," but the "biblical *theologian* assumes that a biblical word as such—abstracted from such particular contexts—has an *essential* meaning."[7] That essential meaning, of course, derives from the unique "understanding of reality" that the Bible holds and not from the vagaries of place and time. Key words, such as "freedom," "merit," "service," "light," "reason," "obedience," "grace," "spirit," "holy," which figure significantly in *Paradise Lost*, consistently maintain their essential biblical meanings even though they may suffer deliberate semantic abuse in the mouths of the fallen angels. The same is true for narrative situations which appear to be as hospitable to secular as they are to biblical interpretation.

Biblical parables, for example, have often been demeaned to the status of mere fables in the course of exegetical history largely because they are deliberately and formally anchored to the realism of worldly experience and seem to offer plausible ethical counsel even though, as students of the parable acknowledge, their essential distinctiveness is their ability to merge natural and transcendent planes of reality. One might assume that many of the most dramatic scenes in *Paradise Lost* share this parabolic potential for religious evocation beyond their literary realism. At any rate, the Bible should serve as an invaluable referee for the interpreter of *Paradise Lost*, assuring him that, as he draws insights from the poem, those insights conform to rules appropriate to a biblical setting.

As we continue to observe the oppositions involved in God-talk (the biblical setting pitted against the worldly, "God" against language, parable against fable, vertical reference against horizontal, and the sacred against the profane), we become more and more aware of its essential contentiousness — the fact that it is a deliberately subversive force which systematically frustrates the efforts of ordinary language to limit expression to the logical constraints of conventional grammar. Even when God-talk takes special pains to ingratiate itself to the natural reason — when it engages in apologetics and presents reason-oriented explications of the faith to unbelievers — it still retains a characteristically contentious eccentricity. To be sure, the aims of Church Apologetics and Systematic Theology depend upon the constants of formal logic to lend their discourse a rigid framework for their operations and by doing so would seem to deliver themselves into the hands of ordinary language, but even here, according to Ferré, religious language persists in its eccentricity by remaining responsive to "informal rules of inference."[8]

Ferré provides an example of such an informal reference (typical of the many that function in the language of Systematic Theology and Apologetics): "If salvation is possible, then God cannot be merely a conditioned part of the world and subject to change." A formal logician, Ferré surmises,

> might be tempted to symbolize 'salvation is possible' by 'S' and 'God is involved in change' by 'C,' and then to derive an explicit contradiction from these entailment rules: 'S implies C and S implies not-C.' But in this the formal logician oversteps himself. It is by no means clear that all expressions of the abstract form 'C and not-C' are self-stultifying contradictions. . . . The informal contradictions are not necessarily self-stultifying but sometimes may be occasions for growth in thought.[9]

One who has given a great deal of thought to the "informal" logic of religious language is Ian Ramsey who finds "logical scandals" abounding in the most unlikely regions of God-talk: theological phrases. Challenging those who would prefer to "establish a distinctive sacred language," not subject to the "general criticism which is applicable to language,"[10] Ramsey contends that religious utterances must never be allowed to sever their connection with the world, that they must always maintain "empirical anchorage."[11] He argues that

> theological assertions must have a logical context which ex-
> tends to, and is continuous with, those assertions of ordinary
> language, for such sense experience is directly relevant. From
> such straight-forward assertions, theological assertions must
> not be logically segregated: for that would mean that they were
> pointless and, in contrast to the only language which has an
> agreed meaning, meaningless.[12]

Although Ramsey explicitly calls attention to an alleged "oddness" of religious language, his implicit point is that it is not so much odd as it is a casualty of the "desacralization of the modern human spirit" that Eliade detected.[13] Ramsey has a healthy nostalgia for the sort of linguistic flexibility in religious matters that Milton and his contemporaries took for granted — a flexibility that tolerated an easy fraternization of material and immaterial realities. His first principle (one which the seventeenth century also took for granted) is that there is more to things than meets the eye, that "we are more than our public behavior." There exist situations in life, he argues, "which are perceptual and more."[14] The whole often turns out to be greater than the sum of its parts, and there is a "depth" to situations for which brute facts seldom give adequate account. Ramsey's position squares with Walker Percy's notion of "certification" in *The Moviegoer* and also seems consistent with Rudolf Otto's conviction that situations, particularly religious ones, carry an "overplus"[15] of meaning, a "sense of the Numinous," which affects us independently of empirical relevance.

God-talk, according to Ramsey's empirical outlook, is ordinary language placed under logical stress, and its method is to "qualify" the things, events, and relationships of the world so as to reveal their depth and subsequently precipitate "discernment-commitment situations."[16] By way of illustration, he describes the shock of recognition in an otherwise impersonal law court when the defendant faces the judge and recognizes him as her long-lost husband. "Penny," she cries in shocked astonishment, calling him by his old nickname, and an "impersonal situation has come alive." Ramsey notes that the significance of the contextually odd word "Penny" is "proportionate to [its] comparative lack of empirical relevance." He concludes that "the situation is more than 'what's seen,' it has taken on 'depth'; there is something akin to religious 'insight,' 'discernment,' 'vision,' " which he seems to regard as tantamount to cognitive significance.

Ramsey's contention is that empirical language is rendered proper currency for divine realities by the addition of depth-producing qualifiers. He addresses, for example, several typical theological phrases ("First

Cause," "Creation *ex nihilo*," and "Eternal Purpose") and points out how in each phrase an absolute empirical concept becomes stricken with "logical impropriety"[17] when it is yoked to an odd religious qualifier. "Creation," for example, is a straightforward empirical notion; it has no religious significance by itself. But when it is religiously "modeled" by association with the curious qualification *"ex nihilo,"* suddenly, "creation" is wrenched into a new dimension. It is transformed from a worldly "fact" into a religiously potent "model" — one in which causal explanations are deliberately nullified in order that a new explanatory context might recommend itself.

Psychologically, the process works like this. The reader initially meditates upon "creation," imagining the variety of creation ideas within his experience: building, painting, birth, and so forth. The qualifier *"ex nihilo"* functions to provide specific religious direction to his meditation. "Creation from nothing" challenges his conceptual logic. He is inspired to develop "creation stories" in his mind, which strive to accommodate *"ex nihilo"* until eventually a qualitative change abruptly occurs — the "penny drops," to use Ramsey's expression, the "light dawns," and he "sees" the religious insight that the phrase has been attempting to evoke all along.[18]

The informal logical properties of theological language, as Ramsey shows us, impinge forcefully even upon discourse otherwise syntactically entailed; the subversive nature of the word "God" proves mischievous even outside its normal logical habitat. But perhaps the most stimulating feature of Ramsey's account is the mechanism he isolates through which the barrier between worldly and transcendent realities is bridged: the theological qualification of worldly models. This notion extends well beyond theological phrases, for, as Ramsey implies, models need not be merely nouns but can also be moral concepts, ethical situations and narrative events. Similarly, theological qualification need not be restricted to mere adjectives. As the Bible abundantly shows, context itself can often provide potent theological qualification. The parables of Jesus, for example, often (though not always) gain their unique hermeneutical potency simply because they are attributed to Christ and occur within the Bible. Otherwise, they could easily pass for fables or mere ethical stories.

For those who, unlike Ramsey, prefer their God-talk exclusively segregated from the language of the world, there is a variety of God-talk which strictly adheres to what some analysts call the "logic of obedience."[19] This form of God-talk shows how far religious language can be taken as a *sui generis* system. It takes scrupulous account of the difference between the facts of observation and the "facts of faith." "Just as our knowledge of the physical world is ultimately based upon sense perception," John Hick explains, "so any religious knowledge must ultimately be based upon aspects of human experience which are received as revelatory."[20] Bertrand Russell, we recall, made the same point from a positivist standpoint when he argued that if there were a supernature, "it would have a structure different from that of language and would therefore be incapable of being verbally described."[21]

Such a logically obedient God-talk runs the risk of becoming cultist by limiting fluency only to those with privileged access to the "facts" of faith. One might argue that Milton seems to espouse such a logically segregated God-talk in *Paradise Lost* when he appeals to Urania to "govern thou my Song, . . . and fit audience find, though few" (VII, 30–1).[22] These lines could be taken as an exclusionary petition, limiting a full comprehension of the epic to a handful of true believers fluent in God-talk. A similarly restricted logic of obedience seems implied in such commonplace seventeenth-century observations as this one preached by John Donne: "The regenerate Christian, being now a new Creature, hath also *a new facultie of Reason:* and so believeth the Mysteries of Religion, out of another Reason, then as meere natural Man, he believeth naturall and morall things."[23] Milton appears to honor Donne's distinction himself when he distinguishes between "right" (or "rectified") and "natural" reasons throughout his works, but the question is to what degree these distinct logics were considered mutually exclusive.

A leading contemporary advocate of the logic of obedience, T.F. Torrance, defends its validity by contending that so-called "objectivity" toward facts is really not a matter of accurate observation so much as it is a "habit or set of mind" which gives the facts their convincing force.[24] Like Ronald Hare, who attributes the convincing force of facts to pre-rational convictions which he calls "bliks,"[25] Torrance supplants the customary meaning of "objectivity" with one more appropriate to human psychology: "the capacity for the mind to be conformed to or behave appropriately before its object."[26] Sometimes, as in the case of facts of faith, the object lies beyond the powers of ordinary objectivity, and the mind, in order to behave appropriately (be "objective") toward such an object, must eschew ordinary perception for one more fitting to the circumstances. For facts of observation, the appropriate objectivity is obedience to empirical evidence; for facts of faith, however, it is obedience to God's word.

One of the most succinct and compelling expressions of an apparent logic of obedience in seventeenth-century literature is the well-known passage from George Herbert's poem "The Flower":

> We say amisse
> This or that is:
> Thy word is all, if we could spell.[27]

Stanley Fish bases his stimulating notions of "self-consuming artifacts" and "letting go" on the logic of obedience he sees embedded in these lines, extending its epistemological counsel to include Herbert's poetic devotions in general. He describes Herbert's language as a process in which "the 'I' surrenders its pretense to any independent motion and even to an independent existence."[28] He builds a case for the "*self*-destructive" nature of God's word, pointing out how "learning to 'spell' in these terms is a self-diminishing action in the course of which the individual lets go, one by one, of all of the ways of thinking, seeing and saying that sustain the illusion of his independence, until finally he is absorbed into the deity whose omnipotence he has acknowledged."[29]

This radical form of the logic of obedience has been criticized by Ferré as "logical docetism"[30] — a God-talk so insulated from practical human experience, so rigidly other-worldly, that, as Ferré concludes, "the value of the human is minimized, denied, and deplored, ostensibly to glorify the miraculous inspiration of the divine." Such language, Ferré adds, "violates the debased human by the divine" and "instead of 'inspiring' the human, assaults and replaces it."[31]

However compelling the logic of obedience might be in the specific instance of a poetic devotion, as a characterization of God-talk *in general* (or at least as it functions in a more comprehensive context like *Paradise Lost*), it is perilously misleading, for by insulating its activity from worldly relevance it drains religious utterances of their dynamic hermeneutical potential. Instead of contending with the complacent worldly insularity of ordinary language and subverting its hold on the natural reason, obedient God-talk simply pleads *nolo contendere* and leaves the field. It is difficult to reconcile the stylistic and logical robustness of *'Paradise Lost* with such aloofness. On the other hand, as one weapon within the larger arsenal of the manifold logic of God-talk, it can often be put to valuable use. Even then, however, it is not always easy to tell whether a pure logic of obedience is at work or instead a logic of obedience merely functioning as one pole of a larger hermeneutical contention. A different poem by Herbert, "The Collar," may illustrate the point.

In this poem a distraught persona shares a powerful vocational crisis, devoting all but the last two lines of his lament to a rational, prudent argument for why he should leave his unhappy, unrewarding position and move on to more pleasurable circumstances. The logic of natural reason is given a full, convincing and sympathetic hearing only to be ultimately overturned by the rival logic of the poem's famous closure:

> Me thoughts I heard one calling, *Child*
> And I reply'd, *My Lord.*

Regarding the poem as a religious statement, obedience certainly seems to win the field, but can the same be said for the *modus operandi* of its logic, that is, *how* the message of obedience is in fact evoked? In other words, is "The Collar" vulnerable to charges of logical docetism? The answer must be no, for the impact of the revelation that the poem's ending produces is absolutely dependent upon the worldliness of the context out of which it springs. In both "The Collar" and "The Flower" the center of hermeneutical activity is not the banal victory of obedience over self-interest, but the insightfulness generated by the encounter *between* them. The point is that genuine God-talk never turns its back on the world logically or otherwise, but rather qualifies worldly assumptions by juxtaposing them to the facts of faith.

The word "encounter" signals yet another characterization of God-talk, one which emphasizes its role as "speech-event."[32] As "The Collar" shows us, the logic of encounter positions the fulcrum of God-talk, not in the ordinary language of the world, nor in the sacredly-segregated language of pure faith, but precisely where the dynamic skirmishing between them occurs. Such God-talk, according to Gerhard Ebeling, "takes living form . . . only within [its] encounter with the language of the world," and he adds that the language of faith and the language of the world "are only what they are in their relationship with each other."[33] The logic of encounter, as Ebeling describes it, is innocent of logical docetism or any other form of logical segregation. "The language of faith," he insists, "is the dialogue of faith with the experience of the world. And the language of the world as such is a confused and concealed dispute about faith."[34] So determined is Ebeling to resist the logical quarantine of the language of faith that he declares that "if the language of faith ceases to be in dialogue with the experience of the world, it has effectively become the language of unbelief."[35]

Donald Evans' notion of "self-involving"[36] language gives us an account of God-talk that is similar to but less contentious than Ebeling's. Here, the problem of mediating between divine and worldly realities is resolved by viewing religious language performatively, that is, by acknowledging its power to change the fundamental attitudes with which we take in the world and experience. Rather than permitting us to assume an ontology that supports such "neutral" concepts as causality to explain events, self-involving language posits a radically theological ontology which overtly acknowledges the *comprehensiveness* of God's creative act. In terms of the attitude in which one takes the world, this acknowledgement forces the realization that all things are institutionally dependent upon God, that nothing is exempt, nothing independently neutral. Just as "the Queen says, 'I create you Governor of Kenya,'" Evans explains, "in a logically similar way the various parts of the universe were given their role or function as they were created by the word." Even our unit of time, the day, is "not an arbitrary human invention or convention," for, "by giving to light the name 'day,' " God created the concrete time of human existence.[37] The logic of self-involvement simply recognizes in a serious, comprehensive way that man has been created with a role and a responsibility. He is creaturely dependent, and this requires that his attitude reflect that status. Self-involving language "performs" the task of maintaining that attitude. Its utterances combine "an undertaking with a judgment. One cannot abstract what is undertaken (for example, as God's discipline)."[38]

God-talk, for Evans, is attitudinal language, and lest we dismiss it as too contemporary, too existential, a notion for the language of *Paradise Lost*, we should compare it with this basic statement by John Milton on the subject of how we are to know God:

> For granting that both in the literal and figurative descriptions of God, he is exhibited not as he really is, but in such a manner as may be within the scope of our comprehensions, yet we ought to entertain such a conception of him as he, in condescending to accommodate himself to our capacities, has shown that he desires we should conceive.[39]

Not God "as he really is," but God as "he desires we should conceive" is the basis of Milton's divine epistemology. Nothing could be more attitudinally based than that.

The key to self-involving language, then, is to translate causal language into attitudinal language. "If we say, simply, 'Jones moves his arm' or 'Jones makes pots,' " says Evans, "our language is neither self-involving or rapportive," but if we replace "Jones" with "God," the comprehensiveness of God's creative act forces a change in logic from neutral causality to creature-Creator responsibility. When all vestiges of "causal" understanding are removed from such religious statements as "God created the Heavens and the earth," we are left with a pure, performative, self-involving assertion which Evans contends can only be talked about in parables.[40] Indeed, self-involving language *is* parabolic language, and its distinction from Ebeling's notion of "encounter" resides in the fact that through performative mediation a divine interpenetration of the world takes place. Perhaps it is not inappropriate to call such parabolic interpenetration the language of incarnation.

Perhaps the most distinctly Christian literary form, and the most illustrative of the incarnational mode, is the parable. Protestant exegetical tradition in particular has been scrupulous in isolating this form from standard literary tropes, insisting upon its functional distinction from such secular kin as allegory, fable, and even metaphor itself (when by metaphor is meant the mere analogical process of saying one thing and meaning another).[41] Christian hermeneutics has generally regarded the parable as an incarnational instrument — a verbal conduit by means of which worldly and divine realities coalesce rather than contend as immiscibles. C.H. Dodd, for example, defends the acknowledged "realism" of the biblical parables by declaring that "since nature and supernature are one order, you can take part of that order and find in it illumination for other parts. . . . This sense of the divineness of the natural order is the major premise of all the parables."[42]

The divineness of the natural order underlies both positions, just as it did for the mystical naturalism of the seventeenth-century Hermetists, which so attracted Henry Vaughan. Perhaps it is true for the parable what Robert Ellrodt claims for Vaughan's devotions: that they are a poetry of "osmosis rather than transubstantiation."[43] If parables are analogical, they are so in a quite restricted way. They are distinct from such systematic analogical forms customarily employed by theology such as *analogia entis*, *analogia gratiae*, the analogy of proportionality, or even, as in the case of Milton's Raphael, "accommodation." The *Cyclopaedia of Biblical, Theological, and Ecclesiastical Literature*, for example, instructs us that

> were we to speak of the word of God as a seed we might be said to use a metaphor, but in that case we transfer the properties of the seed to the Word; the seed itself, having suggested the partic- ular property upon which we wish to dwell, vanishes from our thoughts. But when as a part of instruction by parable we use the same expression, the idea of the seed abides with us, and the keeping before our minds of its actual history, that we may ascend from it into another sphere, is a necessary part of the mental process through which we pass.[44]

The parabolic metaphor never "vanishes from our thoughts" but "abides," thus maintaining continuity with, not segregation from, its referent. In this regard, it resembles what Max Black calls an "interaction metaphor" which has the "power to bring two separate domains into cognitive and emotional relation by using language directly appropriate to the one as a lens for seeing the other; the implication, suggestions and supporting values entwined with the literal use of metaphoric expression enable us to see a new subject matter in a new way."[45] Thus, the metaphoric behavior of the parable, far from segregating divine from natural logic, merges them in such a way that it "is the bearer of the reality to which it refers. The hearer not only learns about that reality, he participates in it. He is invaded by it."[46]

For similar incarnational reasons, exegetical tradition has distinguished the parable from allegory and fable. These forms normally acknowledge a discontinuity between the levels of reality they only artificially fuse. The parable, on the other hand, as Robert Funk points out, does "not lend itself to allegorization because parable as metaphor is designed to retain its own authority; the rationalization of its meaning tends to destroy its power as image . . . .The parable keeps the initiative in its own hand. Therein lies its hermeneutical potential."[47]

Parabolic language, then, earns its metaphorical distinctiveness by dint of its power to merge otherwise logically discrete domains, and what distinguishes its modes from ordinary analogical forms is that the bond between those domains is not essential but attitudinal. The parable of the Prodigal Son, for example, concerns the relation between God and Man, but it tells us very little about the essential nature of God. Instead, it urges that if we look on god as if he were a father, our attitude toward Him is appropriate. Such an attitudinally-based similitude is not simply a matter of encouraging one to pretend that God is a father and to act, therefore, *as if* the pretense were true. The speaker does, in fact, believe that God is like a father, but what he means by this is "to be explained in terms of human attitudes: I believe that God is *such that* the attitude appropriate to Him is similar to that which is appropriate towards a human father."[48] Again, we can savor the consonance of this parabolic logic with Milton's position: ". . . in the literal and figurative descriptions of God, he is exhibited not as he really is . . . [but] as he desires we should conceive [Him]." Parabolic similarities are different from analogical ones, Evans urges, because they are "self-involving" rather than neutral or, as logical docetism would contend, "self-destructive." The parable, in other words, involves one logically in something more than mere assent to fact and something less than capitulation to a logic of obedience. It is, in short, an incarnational mode.

The words "incarnational" and "parable" appropriately conclude this hasty introduction to the manifold logic of words about God, for the essence of God-talk in virtually all of its forms is the merger rather than the segregation of the sacred and the profane. The parable, though formally unique in itself, serves as the paradigm of God-talk in all other forms because in its attitudinally-based, incarnational mode we find the functional ideal of all religious utterances. And yet, lest we presume to reduce the manifold logic of God-talk to a simple parabolic formula, we should savor again the impressive formal flexibility that religious discourse possesses for expressing the inexpressible. When occasions demand an emphasis upon the *disparity* between the sacred and the profane, the logic of obedience, for all its taint of logical docetism, is available. Conversely, when a situation calls for a sense of the sacred experienced *within* the profane, incarnational modes such as the parable stand at the ready. Often, revelation is sought by starkly contrasting attitudes through contention or debate, and here the logic of encounter provides appropriate means. There is no one, single form for God-talk.

One cannot say either that God-talk possesses an absolute, discernible style. Its commitment to the preservation of religious mystery and wonder demands flexibility lest its revelatory potential petrify into literalism. One should be cautious in labeling it metaphorical, allegorical, or even analogical language. While parts of Scripture are obviously metaphorical, there are many others — parables, for example — which are aggressively hostile to figurative trope. What is common to all God-talk utterances, however, is the characteristic semantic duality which the word "God" imposes on it and which makes itself felt in a pervasive awareness of logical impropriety. "God" automatically forces systems of horizontal syntactical entailment to accommodate rival systems of vertical equivalence, thus establishing what David Crystal calls its "'analogical' nature." He means by this description that God-talk "is capable of being interpreted on two largely independent planes. Both planes can ultimately be conflated in the central notion 'God,' but at any one time, either of the alternative modes of interpretation may be referred to."[49]

Crystal isolates what may be the most perilous hazard for the literary interpreter of God-talk, for his words imply that the more successful an author is in rendering secular models for religious qualification, the greater the risk of semantic idolatry, that is, a confusion by readers of the *means* to revelation with the revelation itself.[50] The evasion of semantic idolatry is a responsibility shared by text *and* reader. The text, through its full exploitation of the available resources of God-talk, must strive to frustrate the reader's natural bent for idolatry; the reader, accordingly, must maintain a delicate sensitivity to the various forms of religious qualification embedded in that text.

It would be wrong to think that God-talk is a mere hermeneutical strategem — a mode of criticism, rather than a distinct logical style, which arbitrarily assumes a religious attitude toward *all* literature, sacred and profane alike. It is more than a mere point of view or critical perspective. It is language that shows discernible signs of having been put to very special use. Of course, if that special use goes unacknowledged, no end of interpretive blunders may result. Consider Milton's notorious depiction of God in Book Three of *Paradise Lost*. Read literally, the grossness of the anthropomorphism becomes clearly offensive. Read symbolically, the dramatic immediacy of the scene is lost. Read narratively, the moral and ethical behavior of God is repulsive. But what if it is read as God-talk? What if we conceived Milton's God, Heaven, Hell, Chaos and Paradise not as literal realities, nor as symbols, nor even as metaphors, but as admittedly inadequate worldly models performatively qualified so as to evoke characteristically religious responses in the reader? Then our attention would be less apt to center on the aesthetic or narrative success of the scene, but upon its success in arousing religious awareness. Difficult or perhaps impossible as the measurement of the latter is, it cannot be dismissed as an irrelevant interpretive concern. It is, after all, the central concern of most Christian authors.

Obviously, the interpreter of literary God-talk benefits from the possession of religious faith, but is belief in the Christian God a prerequisite for inclusion in Milton's "fit audience"? Geddes MacGregor suggests an interpretive division of labor:

> The religious work of art has a value other than that which it has for the art connoisseur as such. We expect every cultured person to value Raphael's *Madonna,* if not El Greco's *Agony in the Garden.* But the religious person, as such, however cultured, does not value them very much more than most inferior works of a similar kind; for he is looking not for aesthetic experience alone, but for the initiation of a trend of experience leading towards a union with God.[51]

MacGregor is helpful in this statement by discriminating between the claims of religious vocation and aesthetic achievement. We need to be reminded that Christian literature has a religious job to do which should have priority over whatever other literary intentions it might have. Too often criticism puts the literary cart before the devotional horse. Granting that, can we (do we want to) separate the dancer from the dance with such decisive violence as MacGregor's observation seems to suggest? The aims of art and worship are extraordinarily intimate and interconnected. While we may wish to acknowledge how the priority of religious claims in a work of art unquestionably dictates literary conduct and decorum, we should also appreciate that MacGregor's "art connoisseur" and his "religious person" both suffer crippling handicaps as critics of religious art. Each is blind to the value of the *cooperation* of art and religion as they conspire, not contend, to achieve in their multivarious ways an evocation of the holy.

It bears repeating that there is a difference between literature which is *about* religion and that which is *of* it, and I would argue that the distinction is demonstrable by observing the degree to which "God" destabilizes language by intruding its insistent, uncompromising authority at precisely the point where it meets the most structural resistance: the ontological presuppositions upon which grammar is built. The style of words about God—God-talk—is alive with contention. It shows in such cameo instances as "darkness visible" (I, 63), where the characteristically "odd" qualification of a commonplace model creates the paradox which precipitates God-talk's requisite duality. It shows in the irony of Satan's language which scandalously affronts the logic of his real circumstances. It shows in the strange dialogues between Abdiel and Satan, later Adam and Eve, which are not mere disagreements, but collisions of logical styles which set off sparks of revelatory insight. Most of all, it shows in the overall performative behavior of not only words, but situations and events which are never narrative ends in themselves but always devices for altering attitudes.

Specific demonstrations of active God-talk in *Paradise Lost* in the following chapters will bring more precise definition to the practical ways by which God-talk evades idolatry. In the meantime, three general rules for developing a preliminary sensitivity to literary words about God may prove helpful:

1. *Do not regard religious texts as other than what they are.* A sermon is not a classical oration, a poetic devotion is not an amorous sonnet, nor is a Christian epic the same sort of enterprise as the *Odyssey* or *War and Peace.* Religious words possess a utilitarian charge. They are acts of worship *before* they are acts of art, and this priority makes itself felt down to the very formal structure of the language. "Where prayer is . . . poetry," says Walter Kaufmann, "it is clearly not 'mere' poetry. It has religious significance only insofar as it is not contemplated aesthetically with aloof interpretation. It is poetry in which man involves himself with all his heart, soul and power."[52]

2. *Beware of semantic idolatry. Do not mistake religious models for the reality to which they point.* Religious models, which can be words, things, situations and events, are never absolute in themselves. They are usually limiting concepts like the "available God" — directional signposts which provide only the barest hints of the reality they seek to evoke. To speak of God as "King," "Judge," "Lord," or "Lover" is at best to suggest a human context which might help to trigger an awareness of one small facet of the divine personality. More importantly, moral situations appearing within a religious context more often than not turn out to be religious models (attempts to suggest divine-human relationships like the parables of Jesus) rather than absolute moral dilemmas in themselves. Often we read religiously-modeled ethical situations as though they were mere problems in human behavior and disastrously distort their intent. We must read religious literature with a keen sensitivity to the variety of religious qualification that is embedded in it so that we do not unwittingly compromise the model status of the figures this kind of literature generally exploits.

3. *Respect "logical impropriety."* Confusion, disconnectedness,

ambiguity, fragmentation are usually not flaws but evidence of a healthy functioning God-talk. Rather than "explaining away" the apparent anomalies of Christian literature, we should yield to their potentiality for religious evocation. They are not liabilities but assets, the chinks through which religious insight can penetrate into our otherwise "closed" linguistic world.

4

Hell and Heaven

"What we cannot speak about we must consign to silence."

Wittgenstein, *Tractatus*, 7.[1]

If we should set about to map the linguistic geography of *Paradise Lost*, charting first the semantic deployment of the fallen conversations in Hell (so vividly translucent in stereoptic dualism), next, those in Heaven (opaque in the "absolute metaphor" of "virtual myth"[2]), and finally, the narratives of Raphael and Michael as they mediate for Adam the epistemological commerce between Heaven and Earth, we might begin to understand why Milton chose to open his epic, as he put it, in "the midst of things, presenting *Satan with his Angels now fallen into Hell*" (I, Argument). The language of Satan and his fallen crew establishes a hermeneutical standard for the epic and a point of departure, for it meets the reader at a level closest to his understanding. In it he can hear echoes of his own secular complacency ("Here at least / We shall be free" [I, 258–9]), but uttered within a context made so richly ironic by God's omniscient, totalitarian presence hovering over all that every apostate word jars against an unheard but strongly felt rival connotation which automatically precipitates a religiously evocative *double entendre*. It is not simply that language itself has fallen concomitantly with Satan's horde, as some would argue, but that Satan's language, like the psychological conditions of his exile ("his form had yet not lost / All her original brightness" [I, 591–2]), carries unextinguished sparks of its original prelapsarian meaning — tiny connotive glimmers of lost glory which serve to save the language from the blight of demeaning literalism.

Kenneth Burke might well have the language of the fallen angels in mind when he speaks of the "logological" transformation of terms that occurs when theological words are "de-analogized" and returned to an empirical realm. Noting that words appropriate for supernatural use are borrowed analogically from empirical settings, Burke urges that the

> order can be reversed. We can borrow back the terms from the borrower, again secularizing to varying degrees the original secular terms that had been given 'supernatural' connotations.
>
> Consider the word 'grace,' for instance. Originally . . . it had such purely secular meanings as: favor, esteem, friendship, partiality, service, obligation, thanks, recompense, purpose. . . . [but] once the word was translated into the supernaturally tinged realm of relationships between 'God' and man, the etymological conditions were set for a reverse process whereby the *theological* term could in effect be aestheticized, as we came to look for 'grace' in a literary style, or in the purely secular behavior of a hostess.[3]

Burke cites some other instances of logological transformation such as "create" and "spirit," and suggests that

> if we would 'analogize' by the logological transforming of terms from their 'supernatural' reference into their possible use in a realm so wholly 'natural' as that of *language* considered as a purely empirical phenomenon, such 'analogizing' in this sense would be really a kind of 'de-analogizing.' Or it would be, except that a new dimension really has been added . . . . There is a sense in which language is *not* just 'natural' but really *does* add a 'new dimension' to the things of nature.[4]

It is not difficult to see how the word "freedom" on Satan's fallen lips has undergone such a logological transformation. Its theological connotation as the freedom *to* find self-fulfillment through obedience to God's will has logologically changed to a freedom *from* constraints imposed by such obedience; the "golden scepter" has changed to "iron." And yet, a faint patina of the gold clings to the word, affording it a "new dimension" which deters readers from a total capitulation to Satan's profane literalism. Concluding that "farthest from him [God] is best" (I, 247), Satan seeks to put linguistic as well as geographic distance between his cohorts and God by flattening the semantic dualism that their apostate stance automatically generates. He strives to reduce God from an omnipotent Mystery to a mere powerful adversary by subjecting Him to logical entailments appropriate to creature, not Creator. For example, rather than understanding merit as a value that God confers upon those who please Him, Satan regards it as an autonomous virtue which, in his case, God has inaccurately assessed. Similarly, "grace," for Satan, is not something that is freely bestowed but instead a "de-analogized" act which incurs obligation for the recipient.

Yet for the reader these words refuse to bend completely to Satan's will. Like the one who speaks them, their forms retain a glimmer of their "Original brightness" (I, 592), and the "new dimension" they carry with them assures that the center of semantic activity in Satan's fallen utterances hovers *between* the theological meanings of these words and the debased versions he accords them. The contention of these gold and iron connotations quickens their hermeneutical potential by automatically triggering a logic of encounter according to which (as we recall from Ebeling) the language of faith and the language of the world "are only what they are in their relationship with each other." In other words, they communicate performatively through dynamic skirmish. The contention, not the substance, of these utterances is their essential meaning.

Thus, Satan's "Here at least / We shall be free" is an ontological presupposition which he can keep viable only so long as he can sanitize Hell of all theological qualification. Predictably, the fallen angels "naturalize" their allusions to God by refusing to use the word "God" at all and substituting for it such *causal* equivalents as "Fate" (I, 133), "Chance" (I, 133) and "fixt Laws of Heav'n" (II, 18). In other instances, they favor such descriptions as "the Torturer" (II, 64), "our great Enemy" (II, 137), "Th' Almighty Victor" (II, 144), "Our Supreme Foe" (II, 210), "the Thunderer (II, 28), "Potent Victor" (I, 95), "our grand Foe" (I, 122), "our Conqueror" (I, 143), and "the angry Victor" (I, 169). While the defeated angels do concede God's political control of Heaven by the epithets "King of Heav'n" (II, 229), "Heav'n's Lord supreme (II, 236), "Heav'n's all-ruling Sire" (II, 264), "the King of Heav'n" (II, 316), and "Heav'n's high Arbitrator" (II, 359), they clearly indicate with these terms that they regard God as tantamount to a powerful ruler of an enemy nation rather than as their Supreme Creator. The only epithet in books One and Two that remotely threatens to destabilize the logical neutrality of Hell is Beelzebub's "Heav'n's perpetual King" (I, 131) where the qualifying adjective "perpetual" (like standard theological qualifiers such as "eternal," "infinite," and *ex nihilo*) threatens to "liberate" "King" from its worldly denotation into "model" status. Nowhere in these opening books do the fallen angels utter the word "God."

But despite these overt efforts to eliminate semantic dualism from hellish discourse, they are helpless to prevent an embedded theological leavening from having its way and raising even the most consciously fallen utterances into God-talk. That leavening shows itself in the logological transformations of key words, to be sure, but it also resides in the landscape with which Milton supplies Hell. Murray Roston sees Milton's Hell as a baroque achievement which, unlike "the ethereal dimensions of the celestial battle," is a "more solid, limited setting, human in scale." He surmises that Milton "needed the scene in Hell as a stepping stone to the celestial vision."⁵ Rather than a stepping-stone, I would suggest that Hell's landscape is more like a glass through which we see celestial visions darkly, for even though Roston may be right in appreciating a baroque corporeality in these scenes, there is also a marked *translucence*. We see that translucence linguistically in such famous phrases as "darkness visible," (I, 63) which introduces us to the powerful "descriptive" potentialities of God-talk to "de-naturalize" language and render it currency for religious insight. Here we have a typical example of a model-qualifier situation of the sort Ramsey discusses in *Religious Language*. The logical impropriety it sponsors clearly announces that the descriptive language of Hell is anything but straightforward. Its mode is not indicative but performative; its aim is allegiance not to facts but to faith. It is one mode through which the darkness of Hell is sublimely made visible even to those with only a rudimentary command of God-talk. This view does not contradict the baroque corporeality of Hell, for the empirical models God-talk employs are most effective when their empirical realism is most pronounced. It does, however, emphasize a religious evocativeness that not only Milton's language but also his hellish descriptions possess. The best way to demonstrate this is to suggest some of the qualities Milton's depiction of Hell shares with the sublime.

The sublime is an aesthetic term which, as Edmund Burke informs us, evokes in us feelings of astonishment and terror.⁶ While it is not precisely the same thing theists recognize as *ire deorum* or religious awe, Rudolf Otto contends that "the connexion of 'the sublime' and 'the holy' becomes firmly established as a legitimate schematization and is carried on into the highest forms of religious consciousness — a proof that there exists a hidden kinship between the numinous and the sublime which is something more than a merely accidental analogy."⁷ The aesthetic feelings prompted by the sublime and the feelings evoked by religious awe are both experiences that " 'cannot be unfolded' or explicated," and both are "at once daunting, and yet again singularly attracting, in [their] impress on the mind."⁸ The point is that what we recognize as the sublime in Milton's descriptions of hell might in fact be a potent medium by means of which the reader experiences the holy — a sense of God's omnipresence even in the heart of Satan's allegedly autonomous community, which makes ironic mockery of his "Here at least / We shall be free."

In discussing the major causes of the feeling of the sublime, Burke lists *obscurity* ("No person seems better to have understood the secret of heightening, or of setting terrible things . . . in their strongest light by force of a judicious obscurity," he says, "than Milton"⁹; *power* ("In the Scripture," says Burke, "wherever God is represented as appearing or speaking, everything terrible in nature is called up to heighten the awe and solemnity of the divine presence"[10]); *privation* ("All *general* privations are great, because they are all terrible; *Vacuity, Darkness, Solitude* and *Silence*"[11]); *vastness* ("Greatness of dimension, is a powerful cause of the sublime"[12]); *Infinity* ("Infinity has a tendency to fill the mind with that sort of delightful horror, which is the most genuine effect, and truest test of the sublime"[13]); *magnificence* ("A great profusion of things which are splendid are valuable in themselves, is *magnificent*"); *light; loudness; suddenness;* and *pain.*

Virtually all of these qualities suffuse the landscape of Milton's Hell and the effect, I would suggest, is not primarily aesthetic. What we experience in books One and Two may be more aptly described by Otto's term *"mysterium tremendum"* which, he says,

> has its wild and demonic forms and can sink to an almost grisly horror and shuddering. It has its crude and barbaric antecedents and early manifestations, and again it may be developed into something beautiful and pure and glorious. . . . But though what is enunciated in the word is negative, what is meant is something absolutely and intensely positive. This pure positive we can experience in feelings.[14]

The sense of religious sublimity *("mysterium tremendum")* evoked by such description as "yon dreary Plain, forlorn and wild, / The seat of desolation, void of light, / Save what the glimmering of these livid flames /Casts pale and dreadful" [I, 180–3] functions, I suggest, as a subtle though powerful theological qualification which complements the more overt qualifications embedded in the satanic language. Together these forces assure that the dualism upon which God-talk is founded is alive and operative in Hell.

The opening books of *Paradise Lost,* therefore, deserve their universal critical acclaim not only for their literary success but equally for their effectiveness as religious evocation. Book Three, however, is sung "With other notes then to th' *Orphean* Lyre / I sung of *Chaos* and *Eternal Night*" (III, 17–18), notes which abandon, so it would seem, the hermeneutical potency generated by the logic of encounter so active in the previous books. The two levels of reality implicitly merged in the language of Satan and the description of Hell now appear to collapse into a *mono*-metaphorical anthropomorphism so insistent that semantic idolatry seems inescapable. Little seems to block the fatal pictorial clarity of the "available God," even though, under examination, one can see steps Milton took to avoid this.

Roland Frye, for example, points out how Milton appears to have consciously limited his use of anthropomorphism. "Nothing in Milton is further removed from the visual than his God the Father, whom the

angelic choir describes as 'unspeakable, who sit'st above these Heavens /
To us invisible, or dimly seen / In these thy lowest works' (V, 156–58),"
despite the fact that "anthropomorphic representations of the Eternal
Father had dominated art from at least the twelfth century."[15] The
Protestant doctrine of *deus absconditus*, which dictates that God is
appropriately rendered only through the attributes of the Son,[16] probably
accounts for this, but the resultant "visual *via negativa*," as Frye phrases
it, suggests a considerable degree of sensitivity to the hermeneutical
hazards of *pictorial* representations of God or any other supernatural
item. There is no *via negativa* evident in God's speech, however. God's
God-talk is heavily anthropomorphic. His pettish, self-serving
justifications for His conduct toward His yet uncreated, but doomed
children fail to rise even to *human* standards of good manners. Unless
such repelling severity serves some modeling function (monarchial wrath
awaiting the qualification of mercy, for example), the tactic of presenting
admittedly accurate Protestant dogma from such a harsh personification
seems a poor evangelical risk.

Few readers find much in the words of Milton's God to recommend
them as either religiously or even aesthetically salutary, and the whole
divine depiction in *Paradise Lost* has failed too consistently among critics
to justify any salvage attempt which at best would have to convince us
that readers over three centuries have somehow consistently managed to
miss Milton's point. It may be useful, however, to deduce what might
have gone wrong – to examine the failure in order to learn how better to
appreciate the successes.

Rudolf Bultmann's program of demythologizing the Christian faith
is a twentieth-century attempt to rescue religious language from the blight
of a demeaning literalism. Bultmann identifies language which has
degenerated into literalism as "myth" and defines "mythology" as "any
manner of representation in which the unworldly and divine appears as
the worldly and human – or, in short, in which the transcendent appears
as the immanent."[17] Myth is rampant, unchecked anthropomorphism in
Bultmann's view; it mistakes metaphor for reality and is thus a form of
semantic idolatry. The most dangerous consequence of myth is that it
frustrates the normal operation of religious language by encouraging an
obtuse insensitivity to the way God-talk works. In a word, myth robs
religious expression of its hermeneutical potential.

Technically, hermeneutics is the science of interpretation and
explanation, but, according to Heidegger's bizarre etymology, it takes its
name from the Olympian God Hermes, the herald and messenger of the
Gods.[18] It is not difficult to see why many modern theologians use the
term to describe the special way the Word of God behaves in the course of
transmitting itself to humans. In effect, the science of hermeneutics is the

science of God-talk. In its role as guardian of religious mystery, it is the natural enemy of all mythological thinking which, in Schubert Ogden's words, " 'objectifies' and thus speaks in 'objective' statements about a reality that is not an 'object.' " Ogden goes on to say that when myth speaks about the transcendent power of God, it "reduces it to just one more factor in the known and disposable world. It 'objectifies' the transcendent and thereby transforms what is really qualitative difference from the world into a mere difference of degree."[19] Recalling Auerbach's distinction between epic and biblical styles, we can perhaps dramatize for ourselves the process of myth-making by imagining how the Bible would read if it were re-written in Homeric epic style. Divine mystery would be translated into worldly clarity.

In the event some might be inclined to dismiss the threat of religious mythologizing as a peculiarly modern phenomenon, I ask them to compare Bultmann's position with those lines in which John Donne once lamented the objectifying advances of the New Philosophy in the seventeenth century:

> Man hath weav'd out a net, and this net throwne
> Upon the heavens, and now they are his owne.
>   Loth to go up the hill, or labor thus
> To go to heaven, we make heaven come to us.[20]

What is it to mythologize if it is not to bring divine to human terms — to "make heaven come to us"?

Many might reasonably argue that Donne's lines are an apt description of Milton's achievement in *Paradise Lost* — that his epic is, in Bultmann's sense of the word, pure myth, that it lacks hermeneutical potential. It is not difficult to conceive the woven "net" as the epic's grand-iloquent "answerable style" or the captured "heavens" as a conceptual reduction of divine mystery to common sense, all for the purpose of helping men sort out their ethical confusions. While we can easily understand the mission of the devotional poem as a meditative exercise of the human will directed toward the beatific vision (a willful, howbeit poetic, laboring "up the hill"), Milton's epic, one might argue, is a linguistic kidnapping of the Divine, a flooding out of God's mystery in the very literal light of the natural reason. Something very akin to this view lingers in J.B. Broadbent's complaint that Milton's "normal approach to God was an attempt — like Victorian doubters — to get him down to his own level for debate."[21] Lord David Cecil makes the charge even more explicit:

> Milton was not essentially a religious poet. He was a philoso-
> pher rather than a devotee. His imagination was lucid and

concrete, unlit by heavenly gleams; theology was to him a superior branch of political science, the rule of reason and the moral law as exhibited in the cosmos.[22]

Dennis Burden takes essentially the same view in *The Logical Epic,* prompting one to ask if it might not be profitable to determine, once and for all, whether *Paradise Lost* is a metaphysical system or a religious poem.

I believe that an examination of the conduct of Milton's language in the poem will resolve the issue. If *Paradise Lost* can claim any hermeneutical potential, its language would be the place to look for it. How much discernible God-talk is there in the poem? Are there any instances which can be legitimately described as discernment-commitment situations? Is *Paradise Lost* a truly religious poem or merely a poem about a religious subject?

Until recent years, despite the thoroughly biblical context of its narrative, the "answerable style" of *Paradise Lost* has been largely appreciated as an epic rather than a religious enterprise, that is, it has been thought a classical literary form which only incidentally deals with a religious subject. Perhaps because some felt that this position encouraged essentially nonreligious accounts of what seemed genuine religious activity on Milton's part, a concern for the devotional (what we might want to call the performative) quality of the poem's language began to take root. More and more we began to hear critical interest in the special quality of the style of *Paradise Lost* which set it apart from customary epic language. Isabel MacCaffrey suggested, we recall, that the poem should be regarded as "virtual myth." Finding little metaphoric activity in the poem, she evades the conclusion that it must therefore be literal expression by deciding that Milton must be writing in the mythic mode. "The poet whose subject is myth," she says, "strives to promote . . . not learning but knowledge; to evoke not surprise but acknowledgement; to produce not development but revelation. . . ."[23] Thus, she turns an apparent liability — *Paradise Lost's* alleged lack of metaphors — into a stunning hermeneutical asset: "The myth, far from being a symbolic version of some distant truth, is itself the model of which everyday reality is in some sense the symbol."[24] With this remark she seems to anticipate Beda Alleman's observation about parable: "By avoiding metaphors that may be isolated as single stylistic figures here and there in the text, the parable as a whole is a kind of absolute metaphor."[25] Parables are rooted in the vividly realistic soil of this world; myths, however (at least of the kind MacCaffrey sees in *Paradise Lost*), are products of visionary revelations, and how Milton could have gained access to a revelatory "model" for his God in Book Three is not altogether clear from her account. There are strong hints in her work that Milton somehow claimed superhuman authorial powers.

Anne Davidson Ferry is similarly generous in according Milton prophetic gifts. She asserts that the "narrative voice of *Paradise Lost*" (presumably a voice more elevated than Milton's own) can "envision for us what is beyond our vision."[26] Style is the miracle of *Paradise Lost* for Ferry; it is " 'unpremeditated' not because it is unconscious, but because it is mysterious, more than human, a gift of grace. We are meant to be aware of it, to feel its intensity, its uniqueness, its mystery because these qualities express the poem's meaning."[27] While Ferry and Mac-Caffrey both speak of Milton's style as promoting mystery and revelation, their cases seem to rest rather heavily upon the debatable notion of Milton as a prophet and seer, MacCaffrey doing William Blake the honor of claiming his "vision matched Milton's in apocalyptic power."[28]

William Kerrigan[29] and Joseph A. Wittreich, Jr.[30] place Milton in the vatic tradition and thus their positions bear some resemblance to MacCaffrey's and Ferry's. They sponsor a prophetic Milton whose style in *Paradise Lost* emerges from the Bible, particularly the book of the Revelation. Their work is of great importance in extricating the style of *Paradise Lost* from a classical paradigm and suggesting that its religious content impinges upon its form. Michael Lieb's *Poetics of the Holy* follows the lead of Kerrigan and Wittreich by developing Milton's alleged prophetic stance into what he calls the "sacerdotal" outlook. He suggests that "the vatic finds its appropriate counterpart in the hierophantic."[31] In Lieb we see what might be called a religious anthropological approach to *Paradise Lost* which bases its account of the poem's style upon the works of Mircea Eliade (who examines religious expression from a broad transcultural perspective) and Rudolf Otto (who is concerned to isolate religious feeling as a *sui generis* category distinct from moral or cognitive experience). Lieb is concerned with showing how *Paradise Lost* makes the sacred manifest and thus views the poem as "a sacral document, one that gives rise to a hierophantic outlook that complements and reinforces the vatic point of view."[32]

William Madsen's *From Shadowy Types to Truth* makes no vatic claim for Milton, but connects the style of *Paradise Lost* to the Bible on the basis of their common "mode of discourse": typology. "Milton," he says, "turned to the Bible not only as the source of Christian truth but also as a model of expression. *Paradise Lost* is a fiction . . . that is analogous to the Bible not in its structure but in its modes of discourse."[33] To my mind, Madsen's position effectively tempers the extravagances of those who would elevate Milton's religious vision to mystical heights. "Milton," he writes, "could hardly have regarded himself as a Moses Angelicus who 'accommodated' his ineffable vision to the understanding of ordinary mortals."[34] Madsen's Milton is reassuringly earthbound, and *From Shadowy Types to Truth* convincingly attributes the religious power of the poem's style to "the method of Christian typology rather than Neoplatonic allegory."[35]

Although Stanley Fish sponsors no prophetic Milton, he claims for him an almost equally remarkable tactical ingenuity which has earned the label "reader harrassment." Less impressed by the miraculous mystery of the epic's language than by its calculated deployment, Fish argues that "Milton's purpose is to educate the reader to an awareness of his position and responsibilities as a fallen man, and to a sense of the distance which separates him from the innocence once his." Milton, Fish adds, tries "to re-create in the mind of the reader . . . the drama of the Fall, to make him fall again exactly as Adam did with Adam's troubled clarity, that is to say, 'not deceived.'"[36] If Fish has a major contribution to make to the discussion of hermeneutics in *Paradise Lost*, it is his notion that Milton deliberately deceives us with metaphor and rhetoric only to attach authorial "disclaimers" pointing out to that it was precisely our fallen sinfulness which made the metaphor and rhetoric so attractive to us in the first place.

In the various ways all of the critical positions mentioned so far honor the religious job that *Paradise Lost* is charged to perform — its responsibility to evoke revelation, arouse conscience, and invite commitment. All appear at least sympathetic to the view that Milton's language in *Paradise Lost* is to some degree performative or self-involving, that it is configured to produce religious disclosure and draw commitments of faith. They are generally alert to the fact that the poem's religious content impinges upon its literary form, and yet, they all seem for the most part, doggedly committed to an assumption about the epic's language which tends to conflict with the principles of God-talk at large: that the language of *Paradise Lost* operates as a kind of spiritual barometer, that is, that the spiritual and ethical status of the characters in the poem is revealed by the language each uses. This assumption compromises the autonomy of God-talk by perceiving it as merely a device supervised by the *internal* decorum of the poem. God-talk thereby is subsumed under Milton's literary genius rather than understood as an independent phenomenon of the religious experience.

Language as an ethical indicator is an apparently plausible notion that finds plenty of support from the commonly held convictions of puritan pulpit rhetoric.[37] Plain language, because it is innocent of the artificial adornment of rhetoric and metaphor, is more spiritually pure and religiously appropriate than ornate language which, of course, offers more opportunity for deception and is therefore of the devil. This assumption conveniently justifies the unpleasantness of Milton's God (particularly His monologue in Book Three) on the grounds that He speaks the way a puritan would expect Him to speak: with hard, plain, nonmetaphorical, authoritative language. If we should object that such austere stylistics hardly invite religious discernment, not to mention commitment, we are reminded that we are not seventeenth-century puritans and so cannot judge the effect of God's "epic" talk on the puritan mind.

It is symmetrically pleasing and morally reassuring to know that we can trust style to keep our spiritual and ethical values in order as we read *Paradise Lost:* Satan speaks a language with rhetoric and metaphor; God, the unfallen angels, and prelapsarian man speak a pure tongue. Style, according to this view, polices the internal consistency of the epic and elicits from us an admiration of Milton's literary genius in accomplishing the trick so neatly and effectively. No doubt our admiration of Homer springs from similar decorous conspiracies of style and ethics. But we might ask ourselves, in the midst of our admiration, is this really a *religious* style that we are admiring or perhaps rather an unparalleled feat of aesthetic decorum? We ought to ask this question because the whole notion of language functioning as spiritual litmus has the ironic consequence of pitting style *against* Christian dogma, suggesting (against evidence from Scripture) that the tools of rhetoric and poetry are inherently sinful. From the reader's point of view, the very language in *Paradise Lost* which has been calculated to inspire and affect him most turns out not to be the Word of God at all but the language of sin. In comparison to the enticements of sinful language, the "pure" language of heaven pales both spiritually and aesthetically. God's language has been consciously demeaned for the convenience of aesthetic decorum. Milton refuses to let his God speak God-talk.

Stanley Fish's argument, then — that this very aesthetic vulnerability to "fallen language" convicts us all of our original sin, and that our subsequent realization of our forbidden attraction to it produces a counterprocess of psycho-spiritual self-correction — is an ingenious method for preserving ethical and aesthetic equilibrium in *Paradise Lost.* However, its weakness, and the weakness of all similar rationales, is its assumption that the Word of God is nonmetaphorical, nonrhetorical, and eminently rational. This assumption flatly contradicts all independent evidence concerning the nature of God-talk. Specifically, it conflicts directly with what we know about the style of the most authoritative specimen of God-talk available to us — the Bible. Biblical language, far from being characteristically logical, straightforward, reasonable and nonmetaphorical, is distinctive for just the opposite qualities: its oblique use of all the devices of metaphor, analogy, symbol and paradox. "The Holy Ghost in penning the Scriptures," John Donne preached, delights himself, not only with a propriety, but with a delicacy, and harmony, and melody of language; with height of Metaphors, and other figures, which may work greater impressions upon the Readers, and not with barbarious or triviall, or market, or homely language.[38]

Eric Mascall, in his stimulating *Words and Images*, observes that the Bible's

> typical instrument of communication is not the concept but the image, and this, as Dr. Farrer among others has pointed out, assimilates the method by which the Bible communicates truths to its readers much more to the method of the poet than to that of the metaphysician.[39]

Perhaps even more convincing than the descriptive evidence that the Bible exploits a highly metaphorical style is the utilitarian argument that all God-talk, and particularly the God-talk of the Bible, of necessity *must* be metaphorical. J.F. Bethune-Baker's *Introduction to the Early History of the Christian Doctrine* contains this crucially significant passage:

> All attempts to explain the nature and relations of the Deity must largely depend on metaphor, and no one metaphor can exhaust those relations. Each metaphor can only describe one aspect of the nature of being of the Deity, and the influences which can be drawn from it have their limits when they conflict with the inferences which can be truly drawn from other metaphors describing other aspecs. From one point of view Sonship is a true description of the inner relations of the Godhead: from another point of view the title *Logos* describes them best. Each metaphor must be limited by the other. The title Son may obviously imply later origin and a distinction amounting to ditheism. It is balanced by the other title *Logos*, which implies co-eternity and inseparable union. Neither title exhausts the relations. Neither may be pressed so far as to exclude the other.[40]

The language of God, and particularly the language *about* God, must be metaphorical to avoid reducing divine comment to barren mythology. The Puritan God and the Puritan language that was deemed appropriate to express Him are plausible conceptual constructs, but they present bleak models for the non-Puritan sensibility. They smother all "heavenly gleams" under a stark blanket of chilling literalism.

Bethune-Baker's argument, on the other hand, shows us the absolute necessity of avoiding the temptation to regard metaphor as anything more than a helpful tool in gaining a notion about God. No *one* metaphor can do the job, Bethune-Baker insists, and as soon as we slip from a multi-metaphorical conception of the Deity to a mono-metaphorical one, we have mythologized God, objectified Him in a gross linguistic parody of the Incarnation. Hermeneutical potential not only requires the use of metaphor, it requires its use in a deliberate way.

One critical viewpoint toward *Paradise Lost* which contends that it exhibits the kind of language we have been calling God-talk is that of C.A. Patrides.[41] Patrides is concerned to point out that poetry and prose are radically different ways of communicating and, consequently, that *The Christian Doctrine* is an unsuitable gloss for *Paradise Lost*. Vigorously objecting to Maurice Kelley's "calm juxtaposing of a poem with a prose treatise," he argues that because the poem is "outward looking" whereas the treatise is "inward looking," two very different kinds of expression are at work.[42] Patrides' main objection to *The Christian Doctrine*, which he considers a "gross expedition into theology," is that its language lacks appropriate "oddness" and does not exhibit the peculiar logical behavior of genuine theological language. In *Paradise Lost*, Patrides feels, Milton "burst his limitations as a theologian"[43] and used the kind of metaphorical language appropriate for religious expression. The theological problems of *The Christian Doctrine*, having accrued through inadequate deployment of metaphor, were resolved by Milton in *Paradise Lost* by an obedience to the principles of religious language.

Patrides' indebtedness to Ian Ramsey is apparent, particularly when he contends that the "center of gravity" of the language in *Paradise Lost* is the "model." He is more willing to be flexible with his definition of model than Ramsey, however, conceding that one could use the terms "image, symbol, emblem, icon" or any other term, for that matter, which adequately describes the "odd behavior of a language that is always more in intention than it is in existence and constantly points to something beyond itself." Most interestingly, Patrides points out that "when the 'model' is centrally located, it radiates outward . . . . When the 'model' is abandoned, however, articulation about an insight lapses into mere affirmation in the manner of *de Doctrina*." Models, it would seem from Patrides' account of them, are the primary safeguards of hermeneutical potential. Without them, mythology invades and mystery flees.

Patrides admits that "one could argue that Milton abandons the model in the last two books and in the Father's justification in Book III," but he cautions that "the interpretation of passages isolated from their context is surely a fruitless pastime."[44] He argues that there is an accumulative effect in *Paradise Lost* which works to determine the "center of gravity." Ultimately, that center of gravity turns out to be God's self-justification in Book Three, which Patrides eventually designates as the "basic model . . . designed to throw light on the whole universe of *Paradise Lost*."[45]

A certain vagueness pervades Patrides' account of how models actually work in *Paradise Lost*, and many of his generalizations would be more satisfying if they were accompanied by practical and extensive demonstration. Yet despite its understandable tentativeness, the position is provocative in suggesting how new ground might be broken in the study of Milton's style in *Paradise Lost*. Most importantly, Patrides shows how *Paradise Lost* can be seen to follow rules of devotional, as opposed to internal literary, decorum. Pursuing his lead, we are no longer limited to a single set of formal criteria for measuring the success of *Paradise Lost*, but we can expand our analytical spectrum to include vocational criticism as well, vocational criticism based upon how religiously charged the language of the epic in fact is.

Where do we begin? Obviously the language of *Paradise Lost* is not uniform, and it would be absurd to suppose that it should exhibit a religiously charged texture at all points. We *can* expect, however, that if the epic exploits God-talk at all, it would be most likely to exploit it in the scenes in Heaven, particularly in the words of God Himself. Without necessarily committing ourselves to Patrides' notion that God's speeches in Book Three are the poem's "center of gravity," we can at least concede that they are somewhat of an acid test for all stylistic theories of *Paradise Lost*. Here is the epic at its most vulnerable point. If we can detect God-talk here, we should be immensely encouraged to seek it elsewhere in the epic.

Attitudes towards Milton's God usually fall into two broad categories: those concerned with His literary propriety and those concerned with his religious propriety. It is easier to justify Milton's God from a literary point of view because the defense has more room in which to maneuver; the only thing that really has to be demonstrated is that God's speeches square, more or less, with the decorum of the language elsewhere in the poem. Peter Berek, for example, can point out that

> the particularly stark and 'unpoetic' expositions of doctrine in the opening episodes of Book III give the fit audience of *Paradise Lost* standards for the use of language indispensable for the proper response to the more immediately attractive parts of the poem.[46]

God's language, in other words, is defended not so much on grounds that that is the way God does in fact speak, but on grounds that that is the way God *ought* to speak for the sake of keeping stylistic values straight in the poem. The same logic underlies Arnold Stein's apology for God's language:

> The grand style would be presumptuous, and what Milton aims
> at is a particular kind of bare language that will rise above the
> familiar associations of such bareness with austerity and
> harshness.[47]

Although the word "presumptuous" suggests some respect paid to a higher
decorum than the mere literary, in Stein's account we still see God's
language treated as a strategic inevitability rather than a value in itself.
Even Irene Samuel's reasoning that "the omniscient voice of the
omnipotent moral law speaks simply what is"[48] turns the matter of the
Word of God into a metaphysical Q.E.D. "God," according to Samuel's
statement, is no more than a formal concept; there is no sense of the
holy such as an ultimate personal presence or even absence would
inspire.

Even when such rationalizations of the starkness of God's language
are supported by appeals to puritan rhetorical standards, the argument is
only partially convincing. William Haller reminds us, "We should not
take too literally the boast of plainness in the sermons of the spiritual
preachers . . . . a plain style did not mean for them a colorless or prosaic
style."[49]

Sometimes the defense of God's language as "pure" of all rhetoric
and metaphor strains to make its point. Fish, for example, after
explaining that "in the seventeenth century . . . metaphorical and affective
languages are rejected in favor of the objective style of Baconian
empiricism and the plain style of Puritan preaching," insists that God's
speeches are not "deficient in poetical force" because "in the context of
contemporary attitudes . . . the reader's response to a rhetorical pattern
like this would be emotional, even visceral, as well as intellectual. . . . In
other words, the prevailing orthodoxies — linguistic, theological,
scientific — make possible an affective response to a presentation *because*
it is determinedly non-affective."[50]

At best, the arguments that defend God's language on the basis of
internal, *literary* propriety imply a narrow parochial appeal for the epic.
They leave those who are not particularly sympathetic to Puritan
austerity sharing Broadbent's opinion of God's monologue: "It had been
done much better, in the Bible and the Metaphysicals, and has been done
since, usually relying on Dantesque imagery and human experience."[51]

Can God's language in Book Three be defended on *religious*
grounds? The best way to find out would be to assess the quality of its
God-talk to see if it possesses hermeneutical potential. Certain character-
istics of God-talk are particularly relevant to Book Three, and it may be
helpful to recall them briefly. First of all, we remember, God-talk
distinguishes itself by its semantic dependence on the word "God." We

have seen how "God" words have the power to wrench otherwise ethically-based contexts into striking *theological* significance by their mere presence. We have also seen that God-talk should never be read literally. Finally, we have observed how God-talk relies on logical impropriety to call attention to its unique mode of communicating. Not only does God-talk exploit paradox to the fullest, but it also sponsors strange, idiosyncratic collocations which often result from deliberate paratactical manipulation. Crystal points out, for example, that

> what makes religious English so different [from other forms of English] is the way in which the expected collocability of one item is very often completely reversed from that expected in normal usage. For example, the term *death* in all varieties but this one [precious death] has fairly predictable collocates. Here, however, the collocation is with *precious*, which superficially seems paradoxical, until placed within a theological perspective.[52]

Another important feature of God-talk, not mentioned before, is that it tends to contain a high proportion of unspecific words to which a uniformity of response is largely absent. Words such as "reverent," "profound," "devotion," and "admiration" have no predictable denotation for all people. What one person may believe a word to mean may be quite different from what another understands. Seymour Chatman finds a syntactical vagueness in Milton's use of participles which functionally corresponds with the deliberately vague diction of God-talk:

> So much do Milton's past participles reiterate God's infinite control at the most subliminal level of grammar that their stylistic power is hard to ignore. *The Fruit of that Forbidden Tree* — who forbade it? *The chosen seed* — who chose it? *Satan lay vanquisht / Confounded though immortal* — who vanquished and confounded him? God, of course.[53]

Grammar reinforces the semantic tyranny of the word "God" in order, once again, to wrench an ethically based model into theological significance.

These, then, are the kinds of linguistic features we should be on the alert for as we examine the language of Book Three. To be bluntly anticipatory, the examination will reveal that the style of Book Three appears to descend, reluctantly, from an unquestionably high level of God-talk in the opening Invocation, through a level in which God-talk undergoes evident deterioration, finally to settle on a plane of total capitulation to epic mythology in God's monologue. For the sake of analytical convenience, these three levels can be divided as follows: 1) the

Invocation (lines 1–55); 2) a passage of transitional description (lines
56–79); and 3) God's speech itself.

Let us begin with the Invocation. Here the word "God" appears
directly only two times, and in each case its mystery is preserved by its
refusal to take predication the way conventional proper nouns do. For
example, in neither the phrase "God is Light" (III, 3) nor "the voice / Of
God" (III, 9–10) would it be possible to substitute a conventional proper
name without draining both contexts of their unique numinous
significance. Even "Julius Caesar is Light," descriptively striking as it may
be in suggesting the heroic, sagacious magnitude of Rome's Emperor,
imports something quite different from what the Christian comprehends
in "God is Light." Similarly, the "Voice / Of God," as a performatory and
creative voice (it calls for the miracle of light), has been properly qualified
in context to assure its distinctiveness from any human voice.

The most significant of the *indirect* references to God in the
Invocation is the phrase "bright essence increate" which exhibits more
than sufficient logical impropriety to quality as genuine God-talk.
Uncreated essence, "bright" *or* dim, takes the mind far beyond the limits
of conceptualization and invests the description with a religiously
appropriate fund of wonder and mystery. We will have occasion to return
to the Invocation when we test it for other characteristics of God-talk. For
the present, however, even a cursory examination of its language
discloses its complete semantic dependence on the word "God," a key
religious word which subjugates all others to the rules of its language
game.

When we move to the second level of language in Book Three, the
descriptive passage which sets the scene for God's utterances, we find that
the uniqueness of the word "God" has been compromised. It no longer
seems to resist predicative comparison with conventional proper nouns.
God is pictorialized, reduced to scale. An anthropomorphic patterning
has set in: God is now a king ruling on a throne. Obviously, Milton has
provided us with a model, but the issue is whether that model is "scale" or
"analogue,"[54] replica or isomorph, "myth" or metaphor.

For God-talk to maintain hermeneutical potential, it must retain its
dualism; its ability to evoke discernments depends upon an empirical
anchorage which it can exploit for nonempirical insights. God-talk
functions only within the overlap of metaphorical contexts, and to strip
away one of those contexts is to strip away also the metaphorical "depth"
which God-talk strives to release in its utterances. The descriptive passage
under consideration here seriously threatens to take away God-talk's
double base. The dramatic setting requires a "naturalized" God who
conceptually fits into the *mise en scene*. G.B. Shaw once quipped that in
Heaven an angel is no one in particular. Precisely. If the readers of

Paradise Lost are made inhabitants of Heaven (even on vistor's status)
God becomes for them no one in particular, for His special mystery,
which in fact supports His status as an improper noun, has been taken
away. The passage threatens to make God a super-man, an act tanta-
mount to that described by Donne's lament: "Loth to go up the hill, or
labor thus / To go to heaven, we make heaven come to us."

One could argue that it is the *reader's* responsibility to resist any
mythologized interpretation of Book Three by supplying *for himself* the
counter-context to Heaven that would preserve its hermeneutically
necessary dualism. Satan does this continually in the epic when he
compares his fallen wretchedness with the memory of heaven's glory.
Indeed, the powerful irony of Satan's predicament is brilliantly evoked by
this method of overlapping contexts. Why, then, cannot the reader bring
his fallenness to bear on the scene in heaven and thereby provide the
dualism through which God-talk can properly function? The answer, I
think, is that such a demand on the reader to maintain a strenuously
critical stance in the face of the overwhelming invitation of the epic to lose
himself in its drama is a request, as Peter Berek ironically suggests, which
only a harried Ph.D. candidate might seriously entertain.

It is not all that bad, however, for the descriptive passage is
semantically, as well as narratively, transitional. Some vestiges of God-
talk do persist, which at least suggests that Milton only reluctantly
succumbed to the all-out mythologizing of the third level. Milton uses a
basic model of magisterial authority to present God. He "sits / High
Thron'd" (III, 58), condescends in a kingly manner to bend "down his eye"
(III, 58) to view the Creation, and is surrounded by "all the sanctities of
Heaven" (III, 60). There is not much to distinguish Him from Henry VIII
except for a few tentative qualifications to the model which are genuinely
religious but too few and too weak. God's throne, for instance, is "above
all highth" (III, 58). This is clearly not a pictorial embellishment. Its
function is to avert a too-literal interpretation. Milton seems to be trying
to tell his readers, "This is only a *model* of God I give you, and not even a
scale model at that." The phrase is a genuine logical impropriety.

Another example occurs in the very next line where it is explained
that God "bent down his eye" in order to view "His own works and their
works all at once" (III, 59). Here again is a splendid example of the
religious qualification of a model in that the words "at once" create a
provocative and creative ambiguity which invites a disclosure of God's
real nature: does "at once" mean God sees two separate "works"
simultaneously, or does it mean that "His own works and their works" are
indeed identical? Only a hopeless literalist would want to choose one over
the other because; in fact, what is being communicated in the line is not
information, but disclosure.

Unfortunately, these fine examples of God-talk amount to a mere holding action in the face of the increasing demands of epic formality. The model of kingship simply overpowers the too-small voice of the qualifiers, and God strides out at us from the hazy light of the Invocation with the increasing and frightening clarity of an epic hero. Joan Webber, in fact, asserts that "that aspect of Milton's God which has always seemed most disagreeable to hostile critics, his eagerness to exonerate himself of blame for an event which he knew would happen, is imitated and caricatured from Homer."[55]

There is little ambiguity in God's actual utterances in Book Three. The course and justification of divine action is explained only too clearly. Stanley Fish describes God's words as "a philosophically accurate vocabulary admitting neither ambiguity or redundancy," and then goes on to remark that "God's personal character is established through his language which is conspicuously biblical and assures conviction by virtue of its references to scriptural passages every reader knows." It is probably misleading to imply, as Fish seems to, that the mere presence of biblical quotations assures a consonance with biblical style. Fish points out that there are "eight biblical sources for lines 85–86 alone."[56] The fact is that God's speech in Book Three and God's speeches as they generally appear in the Bible are quite distinct from each other in that the scriptural God rarely, if ever, supplies motives for His actions, whereas Milton's God, as most critics would agree, saturates His discourse with self-justification.[57] This is an important point concerning the semantic control of "God" over the entire linguistic context because the *absence* of motive in God's biblical speeches is precisely that which lends them mystery and thus their hermeneutical potential. Milton, the apologete, however, is too intent upon *clearing up* the mystery. He must have God *explain* the "whys" and, since his God is really a mere magisterial model, the explanations evoke neither religious nor even aesthetic satisfaction. They conjure up instead a picture of a potentate who is not very sure of his ground.

Most of us can share Northrup Frye's ambivalence about God's monologue: reading it as a student he thought it was "grotesquely bad." After years of teaching and studying the epic he found his "visceral reaction" to the speech still just the same, but he could see more clearly than at first "why Milton wanted such a speech at such a point."[58] This is precisely the problem. One's visceral reactions demand God-talk; one's sense of the logical necessity requires conceptual language. Milton satisfies us here only conceptually. He succumbs to the literal.

He does not, however, succumb without a struggle. One of the fascinating features of the opening of the monologue is the striking use of verbs in the future tense: ". . . desperate revenge, that shall redound" (III, 84), ". . . false guile . . . [that] shall pervert" (III, 92), "Man will heark'n to his glozing lies" (III, 93). Ostensibly Milton is merely exhibiting God's foreseeing ability. On the other hand, the verbs display a sensitivity to the issue of motives versus causes. Waismann has noted that

> it is generally believed that an action is determined both by causes and by motives. But if the causes determine the action, no room is left for motives, and if the motives determine the action, no room is left for causes. Either the system of causes is complete, then it is not possible to squeeze in a motive; or the system of motives is complete, then it is not possible to squeeze in a cause.[59]

It is helpful to apply this principle to God's speech because it will suggest that Milton has not been very scrupulous in keeping motives and causes apart, particularly in the instances of the verb phrases just cited, where motive as well as foresight is heavily insinuated. The subtle hermeneutical potential in this interesting use of the verbs, however, is that it discloses the *one unique* instance when motive and cause can be identical — in God. In this sense the verbs evoke a genuine religious disclosure situation.

Unfortunately, the rest of the monologue simply does not live up to our hope that Milton knew what he was doing hermeneutically. As a matter of fact, his overriding concern to preserve Adam's free will involves so much conceptual justification that his insistence upon it inevitably militates against any hermeneutically effective presentation of God. At any rate, these verbs at least suggest that religious disclosure is not an impossibility even in an apparently objectified dramatic situation.

To summarize the argument up to this point, the semantic control exercised by the word "God" displays a diminishing potency as Book Three progresses. While it displays great hermeneutical power in the Invocation, that power gradually declines under the pressure of pictorial demands until, in God's monologue itself, it virtually disappears. The movement is very definitely from analogical to literal expression; it parallels, in fact, the epic's geographical movement from earth to Heaven. The Invocation, for example, is earthly-based. Its point of view is that of a fallen supplicant (Milton) petitioning a transcendent God for "Light" that he may "see and tell / Of things invisible to mortal sight" (III, 54-5). Two contexts are involved, creating a situation calling for some kind of analogical statement. In fact, no other kind of statement except a metaphorical one could possibly express the qualitative difference which Milton obviously acknowledges here between earth and Heaven. As the point of view shifts, however, as we move geographically and descriptively into Heaven itself, what was before metaphor now begins to petrify into myth, for the insight which the metaphor presumably was to evoke is now ostensibly before us, concrete and palpable. The double vision that was so crucial to God-talk is no longer there. As MacCaffrey says, "Milton's world, because it is mythical, is still a *single* world, within which metaphor, as we know it, is irrelevant."[60] The Invocation, however, is *not* part of that mythical *"single* world," and this is why Patrides' reference to the "throbbing metaphors of Book III" has at least partial relevance — relevance, that is, to the Invocation.

We might ask ourselves why some metaphors in the Invocation seem to "throb" more than others. Ferry, for instance, pays elaborate attention to the metaphors of the "Bird" (III, 38) and the "Blind" bards (III, 34–36), finding these images expressive of "the complex nature of the narrative voice — the speaker as limited human creature whose vision was dimmed by the Fall . . . and the speaker as inspired seer whose divine illumination transcends the limits of mortal vision."[61] In the sense in which she interprets these metaphors they are irrelevant in terms of God-talk. They evoke no religious insight but rather "stand in" for conceptual equivalents.

The word "light," on the other hand, partakes of a structural richness primarily because of its theological credentials, but also because it successfully coalesces the customary literal, allegorical, anagogical and tropological levels of meaning with admirable economy. But beyond its direct metaphorical function, "light" is religiously evocative because of its deliberate indefiniteness. The word discourages any conformity of response and, while this may appear a logical liability, it is quite definitely a hermeneutical asset. The denotational "play" in "light" tends to ward off literalism and promotes the kind of open texture which is characteristic of God-talk and which is congenial to individual discernments. Somewhat of the same effect is gained by the phrase "Won from the void and formless infinite" (III, 12). There are no formal limits to this description, and deliberately so; vagueness serves a positive function (perhaps the same function which empty space serves in Japanese landscape painting). A sense of the unexpressed, even the unexpressible, is conveyed through the deliberate obliteration of the very underpinnings of literalism: form and measurement.

In the descriptive section after the Invocation there is some evidence of the deliberate use of unspecific words, but the attendant collocational idiosyncracies and consequent "fraughtness of background" seem to fade away to nothing. Milton does utilize imprecise words like "joy," "love" and "solitude," but their potency for hermeneutical effect is almost completely compromised by their prosaically blighting qualifiers. Exploiting "joy" and "love" as models, the best Milton can do is to qualify them weakly with adjectives that do not evoke discernments but merely suggest an increase of degree. Our fallen appreciation of "love" becomes "unrivall'd love" which we find in "blissful solitude."

Similarly, the potential "background" — the holy matrix which nourishes the biblical style — is no longer background at all once we have moved into Heaven as a specifically described locale. All becomes foreground as soon as Milton seats his God upon the throne; what was in the Invocation a three-dimensional discourse structure now is two-dimensional, a "*single* world," in MacCaffrey's words, "within which metaphor, as we know it, is irrelevant."[62]

The language of Book Three, then, shows us an interesting hermeneutical regression from a fairly genuine religious style in the Invocation, through a noticeably debased religious language in the heavenly description, to a virtually complete capitulation to literal myth. Whatever the literary decorum of God's monologue, its religious decorum is suspect because it fails to evoke a proper sense of holiness.

Although we have arrived at the conclusion that Milton's God in Book Three is a hermeneutical mistake, we have at least seen instances in which Milton's sensitivity to the behavior of God-talk is acute. In fact, it appears probable that Milton was only reluctantly drawn into a religiously inactive literalism by the powerful demands of the epic form within which he ostensibly worked. The verdict, admittedly, is not novel — few readers of *Paradise Lost* defend God's appearance in Book Three — but the criteria against which we have measured and condemned Milton's effort, I think, are. We have not searched out ways in which to justify Milton's God in terms of internal literary decorum (such attempts may, if they are convincing, afford some intellectual satisfaction, but do not erase the original affront most readers instinctively feel at God's speeches), but have simply inquired if the passages depicting Him can boast any power whatever to arouse distinctively religious awareness in Christian readers. We have applied the principles of God-talk as a kind of litmus test and have found Book Three's model opaque because it so successfully "realizes" God as an epic figure that it leaves no room for "an overplus of meaning." To quote Auerbach, Milton's account of God

> runs far too smoothly. All cross-currents, all friction, all that is casual, secondary to the main events and themes, everything unresolved, truncated and uncertain, which confuses the clear progress of the action and the simple orientation, has disappeared.[63]

Perhaps it was inevitable, for, as Auerbach adds, "To write history is so difficult that most historians are forced to make concessions to the technique of legend."

5

Milton's Satanic Parable

Some critics find Dante's *Divine Comedy* more religiously moving than Milton's *Paradise Lost*, concurring with Dennis Burden, in most cases, that Milton's epic is too rationally conceived and "is thus an exercise in clarification, finding system and order in what could, if wrongly taken, appear to be random and inexplicable."[1] If this were true, we might expect the conduct of Milton's language in the poem to be anything but parabolic. Certainly there would be none of the arresting vividness and strangeness that Dodd speaks of as essential to the parable, nor would there be any characteristic open-endedness teasing the mind into active thought and promoting hermeneutical potential. Waldock finds the *Divine Comedy* more religiously fecund because of Dante's use of what he calls the "principle of delegated sensibility." Dante's scheme, he explains,

> had certain inherent advantages, not the least of which was the obliqueness that is the very key and principle of the visions. Just as the divine rays are slanted from Beatrice to Dante, coming to him by second view, so Dante himself, the figure of the poem, refracts to us the sight whether of damnation or purgation or beatitude.[2]

Christianity itself, as a matter of fact, employs "delegated sensibility" when it sponsors the dogma of *deus absconditus*, which insists that no knowledge of God should be sought except through Christ. The divine refraction that the incarnate Christ accomplishes (God's revelation of Himself through the medium of man) does not cut God down to human size but opens to the human imagination His ineffable magnitude. Indeed, the principle of "delegated sensibility" is at the heart of incarnational thinking and, more importantly for our purposes, at the heart of Christian parabolic expression. Through oblique, delegated sensibility

54

God is rendered with a fuller measure of religious sublimity; He is not restricted (and thereby demeaned) by the boundaries of a single metaphor.

But is there a "delegated sensibility" operative in *Paradise Lost?* We do have Raphael and Gabriel, of course, but they are not incarnated nor fallen, and what they accomplish is really a kind of *reductive* accommodation to Adam and Eve of the divine reality, literally redrawing God and His activities to human scale. Similarly, Christ's appearances are not as the Incarnation, and so He lacks the kind of hermeneutically potent doubleness required by an effective "delegated sensibility." What we need to find in *Paradise Lost* is the source of the genuine religious awareness which so many readers claim to experience and which we can assume to generate from some clearly functioning delegated sensibility in the poem. Obviously it must be a sensibility with some very specific features. First, we might expect it to be an entity that can serve as a creditable conduit between the unfallen and the fallen worlds, one which shares the human fallen perspective at the same time that it has also experienced prelapsarian bliss. This sensibility must, in other words, be capable of superintending that analogy of attitude which we have seen to be the hallmark of Christian parabolic expression. It furthermore must be a sensibility that communicates a sense of wonder and mystery by evoking a religious knowledge, as all religious language must, through the medium of man. In short, it must be a sensibility which is fallen as we are fallen, one hounded by God as Christians are hounded, and one, nevertheless, which is aware, as Christians are aware, of the reality, the justice, and the mercy of God. We are speaking, of course, of Milton's Satan. He, I would urge, is the poem's delegated sensibility, its dark incarnation. He is the glass in *Paradise Lost* through which we see God darkly.

Satan has always stolen Milton's show dramatically (sin inevitably possesses more literary interest than virtue), but perhaps a portion of the credit for his exciting presence in the epic can be attributed to his rich potential for religious discernment. That he is a source of a much profounder religiosity than the juridical God that speaks in Book Three is readily apparent from a comparison of the language each uses. Is it not odd that Milton gives us a God in Book Three who, as Arnold Stein describes it, speaks "a language and cadence . . . as unsensuous as if Milton were writing a model for the Royal Society and attempting to speak purely to the understanding,"[3] and then turns abruptly about to give us a Satan who speaks an idiom that bristles with hermeneutical potential? Even critics disinterested in the stylistic peculiarities of religious language sense the obtrusive oddness of the Satanic discourse in *Paradise Lost.* Louis Martz, for example, remarking on the language depicting

Satan's first awareness of Hell (I, 56–9), reports:

> It is a style that might fairly be called *tormented* in its ambi-
> guity and shifting syntax, its abrupt compression. One cannot
> say whether 'kenn' is a verb or noun, whether 'Angels' is a
> plural subject, or a possessive, either singular or plural. 'Dun-
> geon horrible' at first may seem to be in apposition to 'dismal
> Situation,' but the phrase then veers about to become, perhaps,
> the subject of the verb 'flam'd' — or is 'flam'd' perhaps a parti-
> ciple modifying 'Furnace'?[4]

As linguistic bounty-hunters in pursuit of the fugitive religious style,
could we ask for a more helpfully accurate description?

Or take, as another example, Stanley Fish's remark: "The fallen
angels are not altogether unaware of their linguistic problem. Some words
and phrases are too obviously out of place if the pretense of a rational
society is to be kept up. God, for example, is likely to be a difficult word
to utter."[5] Fish, of course, wants to maintain that the divine linguistic
norm is the language of pure reason and that Satan's fall is reflected in an
irrational resort to "circumlocutions and diabolical euphemisms," but
would not the moral insinuations that he makes towards Satan's linguistic
behavior have to be insinuated even more strongly at the Bible? The Bible
too finds God a "difficult word to utter," and the logical improprieties of
biblical language certainly reveal abundant instances where "some words
and phrases are too obviously out of place if the pretense of a rational
society is to be kept up."

The point is that the *literary* view — that Satan's language fits the
internal decorum of *Paradise Lost* by exhibiting a kind of moral-linguistic
depravity[6] — simply does not square with a *religious* account of the
matter. The ideal rationality of God's discourse is religiously sterile; it is a
human, metaphysical construction that finds its model in scholasticism.
The hermeneutically affective language of Satan, on the other hand, has
the stylistic backing of the Bible itself, which strongly suggests that
Milton's purpose in developing it was to exploit Satan as a vehicle for
religious insight.

Hermeneutically potent as the texture of Satan's language is, he is
even more effective as a delegated sensibility by virtue of the parabolic
situations in which Milton places him. The situations I have in mind are
not the blatantly fantastic, allegorical production of the war in Heaven or
Satan's "family reunion" with Sin and Death. They are situations which
are religiously affecting to readers because of the evocative blend of
realism and vivid strangeness that they unfailingly exhibit. Unlike the
allegories, these Satanic parables are not self-contained moral exempla;
they are vignettes which "betoken mysteries."[7] Invariably, they are rooted

in "worldly" ethical dilemmas, but by the nature of their central character, Satan, they inevitably cause disturbing religious insights to surface.[8] In these parables the sacred interpenetrates the secular.

Satan's first speech in Book One, for example, places him ethically, linguistically, and rhetorically in a context of epic heroism. He speaks nostalgically of "the Glorious Enterprise," respectfully refers to God as "the Potent Victor," and rallies his followers with a fitting air of *hubris* and *virtue:*

> What though the field be lost?
> All is not lost; the unconquerable Will,
> And study of revenge, immortal hate,
> And courage never to submit or yield:
> And what is else not to be overcome? (I, 105–9)

This is a familiar, attractive and appropriate model for Milton to use. Kept within a Christian (as opposed to a mere epic) context, it is heavy with ironic potential. Granted, if we take the episode out of context, we can appreciate the power of the speech as a courageous manifesto delivered by an indomitable warrior. But why would we want to? Why would we want to forfeit the religious dimension of the speech by ignoring the model status of the situation? An admiration for Satan's "heroism" can only end in its contradiction by subsequent Christian values and, regrettably, the presumptuous conclusion that Milton created unseemly conflicts between Christian and classical values.

But Satan is a *model* here. He is a model qualified by the ever-present reality of God's providence in the background, not to mention the seventeenth-century reader's natural commitment to the fact that Satan, willy-nilly, is evil.

More specifically, the model status of Satan as epic hero is preserved by the orderly "frame" Milton places around his speeches. This qualifying frame consists of the two epithets "Arch-Enemy" and "apostate Angel" which precede and follow Satan's remarks. It automatically provides theological qualification of the heroic model that Satan's words create and places the speech in its proper Christian perspective. The situation is not much different from the one Herbert exploits in "The Collar" where two competing value systems collide to produce a disclosure and to mark a commitment. Satan's language follows the logic of epic heroism (a bolder analogue to Herbert's distraught speaker, who follows a logic of worldly prudence), but that logic is overturned, in the reader's mind at least, by the logic of theology which identifies Satan's posture not as heroic but apostate. Again, an empirical moral model (heroism) is wrenched into theological significance by a theologically-charged "key" word. In this case that key word is "apostasy" which

possesses religious potency simply because it is apostasy from God that is
at issue.

What, then, is disclosed by this collision of epic and religious
values, and what kind of commitment is encouraged by it? If the model of
epic heroism even remotely invites misguided admiration for Satan from
readers, why not keep him a serpent, a toad, or some other "safe" non-
glamorous entity? Aside from the appropriateness of the epic model to the
theme of treason and rebellion, the reason is that such a valued virtue as
heroism acts as an extremely effective "straw man" when it is ultimately
trumped by a competing theological value. Religious disclosure is effected
by throwing a respected human virtue (heroism, love, honor, duty)
against a backdrop of transcendent theological virtues so that disparities
between them are not concealed but revealed. Ethical heroism is trumped
by religious humility, *eros* by *agape*, merit by election, and so forth. The
aim of the strategy is to break the grip of tradition on the language and
permit it to discover new religious meaning. The old, trusted moral values
take on new meaning and now function within the theological context
that God's hovering presence in the background creates. As we view
Satan within the frame established by "Arch-Enemy" on the one side and
"apostate Angel" on the other, we ought to be attending the entire tableau
as a parable, savoring the conflicts of values between foreground and
background, the psychological tensions spawned by those conflicts, and
the general impropriety of Satan himself within that context. In other
words, we ought not to look merely at the Satanic hero but at the whole
Satanic predicament with its complete range of Satanic attitudes which
we, of course, as fallen humans, share.

Probably the most arresting, strangely vivid, Satanic predicament
in *Paradise Lost* is Satan's soliloquy in Book Four. The precision with
which Milton exposes the subtleties of the anguished rebel mentality — its
vacillations, its rationalizations, its irrepressible flashes of
honesty — certainly justifies the adjective "vivid," and an appropriate
"strangeness" attends the scene not only from the uncanny accuracy with
which Milton uncovers human, simultaneously with demonic,
psychology, but even more from the insistent pressure we feel from
within to isolate the crucial factor that separates Satan from ourselves.
This is a parable of alienation, made strange by its divine backdrop that
signals an incessant obligation which is incessantly rejected. The
"strangeness" is that such a predicament should interminably go on. Satan,
in seeming to perpetuate his hellish status, becomes himself a logical
impropriety. He is a fallen sinner without hope of redemption, and his
condition makes the Christian promise shine so much more preciously.

On the face of it, however, there is virtually nothing in the
soliloquy that is qualitatively distinct from a human ethical predicament.

If we were to imagine Satan as a man regretting a decision to leave a former position, or as a husband lamenting the rejection of his estranged wife, there would be nothing in the speech to impede such a reading. Even the apparent mystery of the acknowledgement, ". . . yet all his good prov'd ill in me, / And wrought but malice" (IV, 48), is mysterious only as the human psychology is mysterious. The kindness of the lover, when one's own love has cooled, often proves "ill." There is more to the scene than a naturalistic account of an individual undergoing a personal crisis. There is a "strangeness" to it as well.

At least part of the strangeness comes from our confusion as to what separates us from Satan. The realism of the soliloquy urges us to identify with his plight, even his person, and yet the stakes involved in such an identification are enormous. We desperately search for some exemption for ourselves from this Satanic dilemma, an exemption which the parable before us oddly refuses to provide. The attitudinal analogy is severely compelling. Its abuse generates a genuine disclosure situation. Our strange discomfiture at seeing ourselves in Satan leads, as it must, to self-conviction, just as Stanley Fish describes the process over and over in *Surprised by Sin.* And yet, we ought not to close the "open-endedness" of the parable so neatly. The soliloquy's "strangeness" is not merely its capacity to provoke self-conviction. Nor is it even in our difficulty in setting our theological status apart from Satan's. This apparent strangeness of the soliloquy is easily clarified by a specific Christian dogma that provides the sought-after exemption that the epic previously announced but here cunningly withholds:

> The first sort by thir own suggestion fell,
> Self-tempted, self-deprav'd: Man falls deceiv'd
> By th'other first: Man therefore shall find grace,
> The other none. . . . (III, 129–32)

An intrusion of this comforting bit of doctrine into the beginning of Book Four would have provided the kind of forensic sanitation which abounds in its source, God's monologue, and would have effectively cleansed Satan's soliloquy of its mystery. Instead of parable we would have found a piece of deductive logic.

But Milton avoids closing this parable's open-endedness, and by so doing preserves a more profound mystery. He does not allow the carefully engineered metaphorical relationship between Satan and the reader to lapse by reminding him of his exemption. Instead, he uses this metaphorical identification to exploit a further ambiguity. He raises in the reader's mind, through the vividness of Satan's subtle psychological self-analysis, the question of how God in fact executes his decrees: is the impossibility of Satan's salvation a consequence of the decree proclaimed in Book Three, or is it a consequence of Satan's own proud recalcitrance which we, as fallen men, can understand and even share? Satan postulates:

> But say I could repent and could obtain
> By Act of Grace my former state, how soon
> Would highth recall high thoughts, how soon unsay
> What feign'd submission swore. (IV, 93–6)

Satan's question is open-ended indeed and constitutes a much profounder evocation of the fallen state than we find either in *The Christian Doctrine* or, for that matter, in Book Three of *Paradise Lost.* Sin is no mere series of infractions, as a literal account of it might suggest; sin is, as Satan effectively discovers for us, a mystery of the profoundest sort.

Satan himself draws out the mysteriousness of sin by demonstrating its imperviousness to logic. We can assume that he is honestly trying to understand the "Pride" and "Ambition" that presumably inflicts him like a disease, because his usual malice seems to be temporarily suspended for the soliloquy. His adversary, God, is accorded flattering credentials. The sun reminds Satan of God because of its "surpassing Glory" and because "at whose sight all the Stars / Hide their diminisht heads" (IV, 34–5). A few lines later Satan refers to God as "Heav'ns matchless King" (IV, 41). He also acknowledges God as undeserving of his apostasy because God "created what I was / In that bright eminence, and with his good / Upbraided none" (IV, 43–5). God is acclaimed an easy taskmaster, deserving of thanks, and fair in the dispensation of His love. Satan avoids casting the slightest shadow of blame upon God for his fall, and his poignant query, "Ah wherefore?" turns up no answer that logic can afford to explain the cause of his rebellion. The careful delineation of God's impeccable qualities, far from justifying Satan's sin, only increases its irrationality. A hermeneutical hole is incovered in the very center of Satan's essence. He is determined by a mystery.

Satan's soliloquy, then, is both "vivid" and "strange." It compels us to apply it to our condition, and yet no specific application is insisted upon or even recommended. The analogical glue that binds us to Satan is a shared attitude which makes the parable seem "fraught with background."[9]

The theological infiltration of Satan's soliloquy is achieved through the standard patterns of religious language. All Satan's references to God are carefully provided with theological qualification in order to prevent literal, nonparabolic readings. In the six instances in which Satan refers to God directly in the soliloquy, the theological qualification is readily apparent. In some instances a theological saturation of the passage is achieved with unusually subtle ambiguity. Take, for example, Satan's invocation to the Sun at the beginning of his speech. He likens the sun to "the God / Of this new World" (IV, 33-4), having already flatteringly described it as "with surpassing Glory crown'd" (IV, 32). At face, it appears that Milton has had his Satan ironically exploit God as a metaphor for the sun (itself a semantic subtlety suggesting his apostate inversion of priorities), but soon it becomes evident that the "metaphor" refuses to know its place and insistently asserts its irresistible authority. The adjectival clause which follows, "at whose sight all the Stars / Hide thir diminisht heads" (IV, 34-5), suddenly develops a deliberately vague reference. Does the clause modify "Sun," "God," or even "Son"? Although all syntactical signals point to "Sun" as the obvious reference, the metaphor, with its suggestion of reverential awe, pulls the attention away from the syntactical Q.E.D. and draws it toward a religious disclosure (already prepared for by the invocation to Light in Book Three) that it is really the power of God behind the mystery of the Sun which causes the stars to hide their diminished heads.

Satan employs the term "Heav'n's matchless King" (IV, 41) in reference to God. The model "King" is qualified by "Heav'n's" which, for the reader at least, should throw the description out of the empirical arena. Satan calls God "his powerful Destiny" (IV, 58). Here God is directly assigned a name which implies the mysterious control of the universe and which effectively averts an "object" or "picture" understanding of his essence. In another instance Satan refers to God as "Heav'n's free Love" (IV, 68). Here God is tied to an abstract model, but the model itself, "Love," is given additional qualification by the adjectives "free" and "Heav'n's" which clearly distinguishes it as *agape*, not *eros*. In line 86, Satan calls God "The Omnipotent." In reality this is an adjective with an implied noun and serves as an illustration of Seymour Chatman's observation that "it is not necessary to mention His name; He is there by grammatical fiat."[10] With appropriate parabolic open-endedness the phrase leaves it to the reader to supply the implied noun for himself: "The omnipotent" (what?) Finally, Satan again refers to God as "Heav'n's King" (IV, 111) which is simply another example of an empirical model yoked to a theological qualifier.

The effect of this theological saturation of the soliloquy is to provide a religious third dimension to the episode, to transform a merely dramatic epic scene into a Christian parable. We should not leave the soliloquy, however, without appreciating one additional feature: Satan throughout attaches to God's action a logic of *cause* rather than a logic of *motive*. Why is this of special significance? For one thing, it powerfully underscores Satan's fallen status psychologically, actually and linguistically. His fallen state is, above all, that of an "outsider." God is no longer a personal entity in his mind but, as the epithets Satan uses throughout the soliloquy suggest, a force. God is "Powerful Destiny" and "The Omnipotent." He is characterized not as "Adversary" (which would imply personality and therefore approachability) but as fate. A God with motives, after all, is a personal God who can be understood theoretically according to human psychology, as a reactor to counter-motives, for instance. But Satan's condition, as he honestly reveals it even to the structure of his language, is that of a rebel without a cause. God is not his adversary but his fate. The revealing disclosure that Satan's discourse makes possible is that his condition is totally of his own doing.

Satan, then, functions as an instrument of divine insight by providing Christian readers with an oblique, parabolic awareness of God's presence. Until Book Nine he is the only character with this capability. Only he has the fallen perspective toward God which is essential to any religiously-affective discourse. Like a stereopticon, he creates a religious third dimension simply by his presence in a situation. To complement the straightforward (and somewhat forbidding) apologetics of Book Three, Satan opens up a whole new range of religiously potent ambiguity and irony. His language is living evidence that the passage from Heaven to Hell is more than a jump from one piece of theological real estate to another; it involves as well a leap from one language stratum to another. I do not mean here a mere rhetorical leap from a "plain" to an "ornate" style, as many Milton critics have ascribed to the stylistic consequences of Satan's fall,[11] but to a leap, to use Wittgenstein's term, from one language game to another. Waismann, we recall, said, "Change the logic [of a certain field of propositions] and the propositions will take on new meanings."[12] Precisely. Satan's words, to paraphrase Wittgenstein, find their meanings not from arbitrary denotations but from the context in which they are uttered. The context, I would contend, is decidedly a parabolic one. When Satan, for example, utters the word "Heaven," it contains an "overplus" of meaning because of the hellish context from which it springs. From a fallen tongue, "Heaven" is charged with a hermeneutical potency that it could never boast coming from one that is unfallen. To Satan, "Heaven" contains a galaxy of meanings which such words as "envy," "hopelessness," "anger," "revenge," "regret" can only hint at. Satan does not describe Heaven and God for us — it would be truer to say that they describe him — but the *whole context* of the Satanic predicament in Book Four, that is, its meaning as parable, cannot help but make the reality of God an intensely felt experience for the Christian albeit delivered through a delegated sensibility.

Of the several appearances of God in *Paradise Lost*, that which filters through the shadowy person of Satan best fits Rudolf Otto's characterization of the "Numinous" and, consequently, is the most religiously affective to Christian readers. As Otto pointed out, the traditional methods of art for evoking the sublime awareness of the numinous have been

> in a noteworthy way *negative,* viz. *darkness* and *silence.* The darkness must be such as is enhanced and made all the more perceptible by contrast with some last vestige of brightness, which it is, as it were, on the point of extinguishing; hence the 'mystical' effect begins with semi-darkness. . . . The semi-darkness that glimmers in the vaulted halls . . . .strangely quickened by the mysterious play of half-lights, has always spoken eloquently to the soul, and the builders of temples, mosques, and churches have made full use of it.[13]

To Otto's list of numinously eloquent builders I think we might legitimately add the builder of *Paradise Lost,* for he too has caused God to speak eloquently to the soul through the semi-darkness of Satan.

6

Performative Precepts

"It is not *how* things are in the world that is
mystical, but *that* it exists."

— Wittgenstein[1]

To the popular mind, "questions about whether the world was or
was not created are questions to which the latest news from the scientific
front is relevant," says Antony Flew, but in the theological sense,
"creation" introduces a quite different set of logical circumstances.[2] Like
"God," "creation" is a religiously-charged word that is mischievously
hospitable to both sacred and profane interpretation. In the natural
world, "creation" is neutrally indicative. Artists "create" paintings, writers
"create" fiction, designers "create" fashions, Christopher Wren "creates" St.
Paul's, and, yes, gods can be said to "create" worlds. As a God-talk term,
however, "creation" forfeits its neutrality and functions performatively. It
honors the active *relationships* between the created world and its Creator
rather than the created essences themselves. In other words, God-talk
regards the "creation" not as a manifestation but as revelation—not
cosmological fact but, as Milton once defined it, "an article of faith."[3] For
this reason, we should be very careful how we interpret the cosmological
passages in *Paradise Lost* and pay scrupulous heed to Kester Svendsen's
important reminder that Milton's cosmology is "a vocabulary . . . . a
quarry of images, not a formal statement of scientific theory."[4] Milton's
cosmological lore is not straightforward assertion but God-talk. Raphael
speaks models, not facts.

In Book Eight, Raphael helps Adam to discriminate revelation
from manifestation by satirizing a group of hypothetical "empiricists"
who, in the course of trying "To save appearances" (VIII, 82) (that is, to
accommodate the manifest motions of the heavenly planets to the
convenience of human reason), set out

> to model Heav'n
> And calculate the Stars, how they will wield
> The mighty frame, how build, unbuild, contrive
> To save appearances, how gird the Sphere
> With Centric and Eccentric scribbl'd o'er,
> Cycle and Epicycle, Orb in Orb: (VIII, 79–84)

Raphael is confident that such "quaint Opinions wide" (VIII, 78) will tickle even God's funny bone (VIII, 76–8), but his cavalier, satiric mood may mask the seriousness of his lesson, for what he illustrates, however ludicrous it may appear to prelapsarian eyes, is a clear case of semantic idolatry. The point Raphael wants to emphasize is that these primitive cosmologists are illiterate in God-talk; they take revelation for manifestation. Coming as this passage does at a point in the epic where Milton most comprehensively develops the cosmology of *Paradise Lost*, we may be wise to consider Raphael's words not only as a warning to Adam to keep his natural curiosity in bounds, but as a hermeneutical caveat addressed to the reader that he, as well as Adam, might be fore-warned of how potentially alluring the "manifestations" that Raphael is about to divulge can be to the natural reason. Adam (but, alas, not Eve) is a reasonably apt pupil, as we shall see in later chapters, but how can we as readers best heed Raphael's warning? How can we assure ourselves that we maintain a revelatory attitude toward *Paradise Lost* in general and Raphael's account of the Creation in particular without succumbing to the temptations of "manifestation"? How, in short, do we read Raphael's narrative as God-talk?

The question is important if for no other reason than an orientation toward the heavens and the earth as mere "manifestation" spawns so many inconsistencies. Walter Clyde Curry, for example, speaks of Milton's "apparent haphazard use" of knowledge in the cosmological passages in which "Christian traditions of all sorts are jumbled with classical mythology and philosophy, with rabbinical inter-pretations of sacred books, with atomistic, orphic, and scholastic speculation, and with Neo-platonic theology in what seems wild disorder." Curry himself concludes that "Milton is an eclectic without any great ability to systematize his fascinating materials."[5] Perhaps the word "systematize" is sufficiently reminiscent of Raphael's perjorative phrase "contrive, / To save appearances" to alert us to the possibility that what might seem "wild disorder" in one logical context may be a quite efficient system of procedures in another. Svendsen, for one, allows for such a state of affairs when he dismisses concern over "conflicting cosmological theories" in *Paradise Lost* by pointing out that "Milton did not attempt a system of natural philosophy like his system of divinity."[6] The very untidiness of Milton's use of knowledge may be our assurance that rather than attempting to "save appearances" in his justification of the ways of God to men, he was actually displaying a scrupulous allegiance to the principles of authentic God-talk.

To speak of the untidiness of God-talk, of course, is to acknowledge that it is a language under logical stress. Since its mission is to express the inexpressible, it is in the embarrassing predicament of having to bully a logically recalcitrant system of ordinary language into addressing itself to realities its very grammatical organization was originally designed to ignore.

Homer's style, we remember from Auerbach's discussion, is clearly committed to "saving appearances" with its "fully externalized description, uniform illumination," and "uninterrupted connection." Auerbach describes Homer's narrative flow as one in which "a continuous rhythmic procession of phenomena passes by, and never is there form left fragmentary of half-illuminated, never a lacuna, never a gap, never a glimpse of unplumbed depths."[7]

No such tidy patterning characterizes biblical style, however. Here we find "abruptness," a "suggestive influence of the unexpressed," elements that are often "disjunctive," time and place "undefined," thoughts and feelings "unexpressed," and the whole, "mysterious and 'fraught with background.' "[8] Even the surface texture of God-talk reveals its commitment to a sacred ontology. Its deep structure reveals a reference system that is always oriented to God's will rather than the neutral manifestations of nature. Its function, therefore, is not to inform but to *perform* — to change human attitudes rather than provide facts. Once the logical conduct of God-talk is understood, Milton's alleged "haphazard" use of knowledge, no matter how disordered it may seem to standards of conventional reason, cannot be dismissed as a violation of logic; it is, rather, an organization of knowledge based upon a logic other than that to which many of us may be accustomed.

Raphael's lectures to Adam on the cosmos make no sense as natural science. Svendsen, among others, effectively demonstrates that what Raphael describes "is not even a proper system, for although its static outline is Ptolemaic, the celestial motions are not harmonized — indeed the mode of the poem capitalizes upon their imprecision."[9] Imprecision indeed. Raphael exploits an accumulated mass of patently inconsistent cosmological information (which is irrelevant to his real pedagogical purposes with Adam) in order to evoke in his student a proper awareness of his true ontological status: one of creaturely dependence upon his omnipresent Creator. Through consistently in-consistent "miss-sayings" about the cosmos, Raphael pointedly renders rather than explains the truth of Herbert's admonishment in "The Flower":

We say amisse
This or that is:
Thy word is all, if we could spell.

In the prelapsarian context of Book Eight, the logic of obedience illustrated in these lines is perfectly appropriate to Raphael's purposes. His words are not informative, but performative. They seek to effect and maintain a "right" relationship between Adam and his Creator. In short, Raphael speaks a pure, prescriptive God-talk; he consistently admonishes Adam of "appearances" and recommends in their place an attitude he *ought* to hold toward phenomena — that they are God's achievements. In every instance Raphael diverts Adam from scientism to devotion. Recall how he pointedly remarks, ". . . whether Heav'n move or Earth, / Imports not, if thou reck'n right" (VIII, 70–1). "Right" reckoning ignores such "quaint Opinions wide" as to whether the cosmos is Ptolemaic or Copernican, for it knows they are irrelevant, potentially idolatrous strategies for "saving appearances." Right reckoning dictates that Adam "ought / Rather admire" (VIII, 74–5); he is enjoined to strike a religiously appropriate attitude rather than to indulge his uncommitted curiosity.

Another example of Raphael's nonscientistic persuasion is his observation that although physical size and intensity usually infer an apparent value in things, true value (if "reck'nd right" is ultimately conferred by "The Maker's high magnificence" (VIII, 101):

> consider first, that Great
> Or Bright infer not Excellence: the Earth
> Though, in comparison of Heav'n, so small,
> Nor glistening, may of solid good contain
> More plenty than the Sun that barren shines,
> Whose virtue on itself works no effect,
> But in the fruitful Earth; there first receiv'd
> His beams, unactive else, thir vigor find.
> Yet not to Earth are those bright Luminaries
> Officious, but to thee Earth's habitant. (VIII, 90–9)

According to Raphael's criteria, excellence is measured in performance rather than essence. The sun gains its value not from its "barren" self but from what it *does* to "fruitful Earth." Similarly, Earth derives its value from the fact that it houses Man. Values are not inherent; they are assigned. The Heavens, for instance, are "spacious," Raphael explains,

> That Man may know he dwells not on his own;
> An edifice too large for him to fill, . . .
> Ordain'd for uses to his Lord best known (VIII, 102–06)

In Book Seven he praises Adam's "caution" (VII, 111) in stating the motive behind his curiosity as "the more / To magnify his works" (VII, 96–7), and he is careful to limit his own remarks to that "which best may serve / To glorify the Maker" (VII, 115–16). Devotion ("right" reckoning), not scientism, is Raphael's consistent aim. So far is scientism from Raphael's concern that he repeatedly goes out of his way to remind Adam that his explanations are really only useful fictions. On one occasion he wants to be sure that Adam attribute the "swiftness of those Circles" (the orbits of the planets) to God's "Omnipotence" (VIII, 107–08) rather than natural causes, but he finds that this requires that he admit "Motion in the Heav'ns" (VIII, 115), an accommodation which he, interestingly, considers spurious, since he immediately qualifies it with "Not that I so affirm, though so it seem / To thee who hast thy dwelling here on earth" (VIII, 117–18). Raphael's zeal to promote "right" reckoning supercedes any concern for literal accuracy, an indication that his remarks are directed less to the reason than to "the *heart* of man" [italics added] (VII, 114).

If this were an isolated instance, it might not carry much weight as a clue to Milton's religious strategy in the creation passages of *Paradise Lost*. The fact is that Raphael curiously accommodates all the hexameral material to Adam when there seems no apparent reason to accommodate at all. "Immediate are the Acts of God," he says, "more swift / Than time or motion, but to human ears / Cannot without process of speech be told" (VII, 176–78). He speaks like the early Christian Platonists, who believed that the works of the days was merely a manner of revealing the creation and not a literal account in Genesis, that, in fact, the world was actually created in an instant but described to men in terms of time and motion. With Raphael, at least, Milton adopts a position that is different from virtually all of his contemporary Protestant and Catholic exegetes. In his account of the commentaries on Genesis from 1572–1633, Arnold Williams says, "With the single exception of Brocardus, every commentator I have read is determined that the Mosaic account be taken literally."[10] Raphael's accommodated version is all the more difficult to explain when we recall that Milton himself in *The Christian Doctrine* does not deny that time and motion "existed before this world was made."[11] Why, we wonder, does Milton have Raphael make such a point of insisting that his account of the Creation is an accommodation when his "accommodated" version is essentially no different than Moses' literal report in Genesis?

Perhaps the tactic offered Milton some needed artistic flexibility, some additional elbow room which the terse, biblical *donnée* denied. An "accommodated" version of the Creation would not be held as strictly to account as one which presumed to be literal history. Perhaps, but there are more compelling *hermeneutical* reasons for Milton's apparently unnecessary accommodation of literal history. One is that it allowed him to avoid the problem to which he had succumbed in the presentation of God in Book Three. There, the hermeneutical failure resulted from a rejection of the "double-vision" that characterizes a healthy, functioning God-talk. The "otherness" of God was compromised, making Him vulnerable to human standards of judgment. Even more importantly, the performative nature of God-talk was forfeited, making it difficult, though not impossible to take God's speech as anything but an unsatisfactory "saving of appearances." Had God's appearance in Book Three been "accommodated," it is unlikely that it would be as vulnerable to deserved criticism as it is.

But of course the Bible itself "accommodates" its depictions of God and most other transcendent entities, as Milton's statement on our knowledge of God attests (God condescends "to accommodate himself to our capacities"), for if it did not, its language would be void of any religiously affecting power. The important thing to understand is the *nature* of that biblical accommodation, which Milton makes very clear in his statement: we know God not "as he really is" but as "he desires we should conceive." Attitude, not essence, binds biblical analogues, just as we shall see it binds the analogues in Raphael's accommodated language. Such analogies, if they can be called that, are not pedagogical but devotional instruments. Their function is to manipulate the human will – to affect attitudes – and evoke, performatively, religious discernments. This kind of performative evocation is a biblical staple, and I believe its proper nomenclature is neither analogy nor accommodation but parable.

We can recall from Chapter Three that the fundamental employment of the parable is to precipitate a religious disclosure which effects an interpenetration of divine and worldly realities. Unlike myth, which Trophime Mouiren says "encompasses in the same world, in the same sphere, man and the gods,"[12] parabolic stories of creation "mark a difference in plane, a rupture between the given world and the domain of reality that is in no sense continuous with the world."[13] If it can be granted that Raphael's "accommodated" account of the Creation is a parabolic rendering, we will be interested to know *how* the parable achieves the merger of otherwise discontinuous realities. To that end we should take a closer look at C.H. Dodd's classic definition. The parable, he says, is a "metaphor or simile" which, among other things, "arrests" the hearer by its "vividness and strangeness . . . leaving the mind in sufficient doubt about its precise application to tease it into active thought."[14] Unlike analogy, which generally compares essentials, the parable strives to effect a mental state rather than form an inference; "active thought" rather than any final conclusion is its goal. A father joyously welcomes home his prodigal son, illustrating the appropriateness of the son's trust in his father's forgiveness. Although God is qualitatively different from the mortal father in every tangible way (He is transcendent), the parable urges (with biblical authority) a similarity not of feature, dimension nor any other worldly category, but of attitude and attitude alone. Our trust in God's forgiveness of sinners should be the same as a son's trust in his father's forgiveness. As mentioned in Chapter One, parabolic analogies are independent of the traditional analogical modes of the scholastics: "attribution," "proportionality," and even "being."[15] The biblical parable honors divine transcendence more completely by "relating" divine and worldly realities exclusively in terms of scripturally provoked and scripturally authorized human *attitudes*. The analogues of parable are bonded by no manifest commonality but by the sheer force of God's *will* (as "he desires we should conceive") as revealed in the Word of God. In short, biblical parables do not describe; they *pre*scribe an attitude according to which the devotee is urged to look on himself, the world and God.

If Milton intended Raphael's version of the Creation as a parable (as his insistence that it be an "accommodated" rendering suggests), then our quest for what happens religiously in *Paradise Lost* is greatly furthered by regarding Raphael's words as recommendations as to how Adam (and the readers of *Paradise Lost*) ought to "look on" his theological status. Recalling Donald Evans' observation that when " 'I look on *x* as *y*,' I commit myself to a policy of behavior and thought and I register my decision that *x* is appropriately described as *y*," we can see that Raphael's speech "combines an undertaking with a judgment."[16] It is true, as Evans is quick to concede, that some onlooks behave like ordinary metaphors and are clearly analogical rather than parabolic; parabolic onlooks, however, like Raphael's, enjoy currency only within a context of attitudes and bear no other common relationship. To clarify the distinction between analogical and parabolic onlooks, Evans provides a list of examples:

> (I) 'I look on Henry as a brother.'
> 'I look on Smith as a tool.'
> 'I look on the vicar as my shepherd.'
> (II) 'I look on music as a language.'
> 'I look on alcoholism as a disease.'
> 'I look on Adenauer as the architect of the new Germany.'

The first group are parabolic onlooks, for "the similarity which is implied between *x* and *y* is mainly in terms of appropriate attitude: *x* is *such that* the attitude appropriate to *y* is similar to the attitude appropriate to *x*." In the second group, however, a similarity is assumed between *x* and *y* "which is independent of any similarity of appropriate attitude. The meaning of 'I look on *x* as *y*' can here be readily analyzed by abstracting a content (for example, 'alcoholism is a disease') and then adding autobiographical and commissive elements." Onlooks of this type are analogical because they possess a more or less neutral core of content which serves to bond the analogues. Parabolic onlooks have no such neutral core of content and the common bond between the analogues is restrictively attitudinal.

Evans concedes that "it would be difficult to establish conclusively that, of all the many ways in which the Bible indicates God's transcendence, none provide a genuine analogy and all are parabolic," but he admits that "he is inclined to think that this is so."[17] Certainly Milton's position that we know God not "as he really is" but "as he desires we should conceive [Him]" powerfully suggests his intuitive awareness of the parabolic nature of God-talk, but perhaps the most convincing evidence that the logical structure of God-talk (be it biblical or Miltonic) is parabolic is that the reading of the world it sponsors is itself a parabolic onlook: "I look on the world as God's creation." Biblical God-talk is totally reliant on onlooks (often inconsistent and contradictory) for the exclusive purpose of urging an appropriate attitude toward God within different contexts. Sometimes, as we have seen, God is a shepherd, other times a potter, a father, an architect, etc., depending upon how God "desires we should conceive [Him]" in each situation. The Bible does not recommend pragmatically that one act *as if* he believed God were a shepherd, a potter, a father, or an architect. The devotee is called upon actually to believe God is like these beings, but what is meant by these onlooks can be explained *only* in terms of human attitudes: one believes that God is *such that* the attitude appropriate to Him is similar to that which is appropriate towards a human father, shepherd, potter and architect. Parabolic expressions, therefore, are not mere analogies, metaphors, allegories or myths; they are faith expressions. Religious commitment is essential to their structure, for their verification rests not in any essential resemblance between sacred and profane elements but solely in one's committed trust that this is how God "desires we should conceive."

If I urge, then, that Raphael's cosmogony and his hexameral account (both consistent with Scripture) follow less the logic of cosmology or even epic narration than they do the parabolic patterning of God-talk, I am not advancing any novel claim about Milton's stylistic inventiveness; I am merely acknowledging a biblical legacy.

Evans' formula, "I look on *x* as *y*," seems to me an unusually efficient tool for demonstrating what is going on *religiously* in *Paradise Lost*, for its total commitment to the *performative* forces operating in

Milton's language compels us to observe Christian rather than aesthetic priorities in our interpretations. Whatever incidental scientific or even moral import Raphael's "explanations" might contain, the *religious* impact of his narrative — its primary intention — is best appreciated and devotionally savored as a series of parabolic onlooks, onlooks which are directly recommended to Adam but which are also aimed at the religiously sensitive reader of *Paradise Lost*.

Let us begin with some obvious instances. Raphael reports God's instructions to Christ:

> And thou my Word, begotten Son, by thee
> This I perform, speak thou, and be it done: (VII, 163–64)

Taken as a "self-involving" parabolic onlook — as God-talk — this passage generates an almost endless string of religious insights, particularly because of the resonance of the key religious term "Word":

> I look on Christ as the Word of God.
> I look on the Word (Christ, the Scriptures) as the instrument of Creation.
> I look on the Word as an instantaneous effecter of creative change.
> I look on the Word as God's performative mode.
> I look on Creation as a verbal activity.

Subsidiary insights might develop in these ways:

> I look on Creation as a hearing of the Word.
> I look on Words as divinely performative.

which will lead us once again to Herbert's discernment in "The Flower": "We say amisse, / This or that is: / Thy word is all, if we could spell."

More controversial is this passage:

>   I am who fill
> Infinitude, nor vacuous the space.
> Though I uncircumscrib'd myself retire,
> And put not forth my goodness, which is free
> To act or not . . . (VII, 168–72)

No doubt the controversy over Milton's alleged materialism and his refusal to accept the conventional view of creation *ex nihilo* have eclipsed the parabolic significance of passages like this one, but once again Evans' formula efficiently exposes its religious yield:

I look on God as omnipresent.
I look on Infinitude as alive with divine presence.
I look on uncreated chaos as the absence of God's creative
  presence.

Raphael further reports that "The King of Glory in his powerful Word /
And Spirit" (VII, 208-9) surveys the "vast immeasurable Abyss" of the
chaos from which the world will be created and regards it as

Outrageous as a Sea, dark, wasteful, wild
Up from the bottom turn'd by furious winds
And surging waves, as Mountains to assault
Heav'ns highth, and with the Centre mix the Pole. (VII, 212-15)

Here is an onlook which richly characterizes a state from which
God has retired and ceased putting forth His goodness. I look on the
absence of God as discord, the formula dictates, and Milton immediately
provides the parabolic remedy:

Silence, ye troubl'd waves, and thou Deep, peace
Said then th' Omnific Word, your discord end. (VII, 216-7)

The issue of Milton's "materialism" in the context of these passages is
religiously irrelevant and scientifically absurd. The "matter" that Raphael
describes is, by any account other than parabolic, odd, to say the least.
"Matter unform'd and void" (VII, 233), he mysteriously calls it, which is
as much a scandal to the natural reason as the famous earlier reference to
the "darkness visible" (I, 63) of Hell. Ian Ramsey would seize on both
expressions as characteristically religious discernment-commitment
situations in which empirical models ("matter" and "darkness") are
theologically qualified (and thus rendered empirically "odd") by illogical
adjectives ("unform'd and void" and "visible").[18] Such religiously-
qualified models achieve the parabolic goal of effecting the
interpenetration of worldly and divine realities within the context of
human attitudes. Ramsey himself uses the phrase "creation *ex nihilo*" as
his example in which the word "creation" is wrenched into a new
dimension, one in which causal explanations are deliberately nullified in
order that a new explanatory context might recommend itself. Milton's
"Matter unform'd and void" insists upon parabolic interpretation of the
sort Evans' formula again precipitates: I look on matter as unformed and
void until "created" by the Word.
　　The same insight is evoked by Raphael's parable of the Creator-
Word as a divine draftsman:

> He took the golden Compasses, prepar'd
> In God's Eternal store, to circumscribe
> This universe, and all created things,
> One foot he centred, and the other turn'd
> Round through the vast profundity obscure,
> And said, Thus far extend, thus far thy bounds,
> This be thy just Circumference, O World. (VII, 225–31)

The parable urges that we "look on" the world as circumscribed by the Word of God and that beyond the circumference of the circle of perfection, which the Word in all its Christian senses etches, lies only a limitless darkness, a "vast profundity obscure."

One of the more prominent creation parables that Evans isolates is that of the Victor. Exegetical tradition has seen the creation of the firmament and shore as "God's barriers against the menace of the waters," and has interpreted the creation of light as a parallel defense against the "vast profundity obscure" which, as Evans notes, "might otherwise have merged chaotically with it." Of course in the Bible and in *Paradise Lost* light is not so much created (God Himself, after all, is the "fountain of light") as it is given various forms. Its first created form, we recall, is as "Light / Ethereal, first of things, quintessence pure . . . Sphere'd in a radiant Cloud, for yet the Sun / Was not" (VII, 243, 247). Considered nonparabolically, there is an obvious puzzle (among others) of why a "radiant Cloud" should precede the subsequently created sun, thereby intruding a confusing complication into an otherwise systematic creation account. Obviously, the intention of Scripture and *Paradise Lost* is to use light parabolically, as a means of orienting human attitudes toward God's will. The believer is urged to 'look on" light in a rich variety of spiritually salutary ways:

> I look on light as my Creator who is the "fountain of light."
> I look on light as a victory over the darkness of chaos.
> I look on light as God's Word protecting me from the "vast pro-
>   fundity obscure."

None of these claims for light would hold if light were permitted to become the ontological captive of Nature, but Milton and Scripture take pains to insure that it retain its significance as sign (VII, 341) and serve as a demonstration of the divine *attitude* toward Creation rather than a created thing in itself. Light emanates from God, "the fountain of light," not from the created sun, nor even originally from the "radiant Cloud" (VII, 247). Eventually, of course, light is 'Transplanted from her cloudy Shrine, and plac'd / In the Sun's Orb, made porous to receive / And drink the liquid Light" (VII, 360–62), but the entire process is tantamount to incarnation, and its performative force is to stress parabolically God's active presence in His Creation. Even God's creating words, "Let there be Light, and forthwith Light / Ethereal, . . . God saw the light was good" (VII, 243–49) demonstrate the will of God functioning through Light as Creator, Victor, Administrator of Natural Process and even as Assigner of Value. As a richly suggestive parabolic onlook, Light speaks to the believer as the victory of God's performative Word over the "vast profundity obscure" of disorder, chaos and meaninglessness.

The parables of creation reveal an ontological tension that afflicts all of *Paradise Lost*. Svendsen calls it a "dualism of order and restraint . . . [an] ultimate conflict between law and nature," and he pinpoints the conflict by juxtaposing two Miltonic statements: ". . . the light of grace [is] a better guide than Nature" *(Animadversions)* and "God and nature bid the same" (VI, 176)."[19] Appearances would seem to support a decided "ambivalence" in Milton's poem in which man's determination that "this or that is" made to collide with God's "Word." But as with all Christian paradoxes, the resolution simply awaits acquiescence to dogma. One of the more controversial remarks which Raphael attributes to God is a case in point:

> Necessity and Chance
> Approach not mee, and what I will is Fate. (VII, 172–73)

The words strike us as harshly deterministic in this naked form, and yet their meaning is no different from "God and Nature bid the same." A "metaphysical" reading delivers a different insight than a religious one, for how richly does this perplexing utterance, when taken as an "onlook," yield providential comfort rather than predestinational resignation. Not only do these words reconcile nature and grace by appropriating determinism under the banner of Providence, but they also urge that the apparent determinism of God be looked on instead as His pledge of consistency. God's will *is* Fate because He chooses to pledge it so. In other words, read as God-talk, this passage is a covenantal utterance. The regularity of the created cosmos — the consistency of the Law of Nature — is a divine promise. If God and Nature appear not "to bid the same," as often is the case in *Paradise Lost* and Scripture, the fault lies in man's attitude — his refusal to regard his home in Creation as "revelation" rather than "manifestation." Again, Herbert, with typical Protestant insight, captures precisely the ideal of the logic of obedience which in the innocence of prelapsarian Eden is supremely appropriate, even though as a postlapsarian linguistic mode it deserves the charge of logical docetism: "Thy word is all, if we could spell."

7

Mammon, Models and Militancy

A man that looks on glass,
On it may stay his eye,
Or, if he pleaseth, through it pass,
And then the heaven espy.
                                    — George Herbert[1]

A genuinely Christian epic ought to meet the logical requirements of faith as well as reason, and I think *Paradise Lost* does. Such a position sometimes conflicts with other points of view which do not take as seriously the fact that faith and reason seldom mix without mutual compromise. The most serious threat to a genuinely Christian *Paradise Lost* is the view that sees the epic bearing an obligation to display a uniformly consistent, rational coherence, a view, in other words, that honors the requirements of reason at the expense of faith.

The contention of reason and faith in terms of logic is a kind of territorial dispute over cognitive domains. The natural logic claims cognitive jurisdiction over the empirical universe and walls it in with the bricks and mortar of syllogism lest such "emotive" impurities as religious faith should infiltrate. It refuses to recognize the cognitive validity of nonempirical (thus nonverifiable) propositions. Faith, on the other hand, subversively seeks to liberate "knowledge" from such a barren prison by deliberately subverting the syllogistic walls in order to let in fresh cognitive air. Owen Barfield once expressed the inherent cognitive restrictiveness of natural logic this way:

> The logical use of language presupposes the meanings of the words it employs and presupposes them constant. I think it will be found a corollary of this that the logical use of a language can never add any meaning to it. The conclusion of a syllogism

is implicit already in the premises, that is, in the *meanings* of *words* employed.²

Philip Wheelwright has invented the term "steno-language" to describe the logical use of language that Barfield discusses. "Steno-language," Wheelwright contends, "has the cold purity that comes from adherence to rules; and ultimately there is but a single kind of logical purity, the set ideal of all logical thinking."³ Steno-language in its purest and most pernicious form appears in Orwell's *1984* as "Newspeak," but even in its hybrid varieites it yields the picture of a linguistic prison constructed of bricks of petrified denotation and the mortar of syllogism. It is a "closed" and complacent linguistic world which permits the entrance of no new knowledge. It is a language environment pledged to linguistic. agnosticism.

Dennis Burden's *The Logical Epic* surely does not regard *Paradise Lost* as Orwellian Newspeak, but it does its best to convince us that its logical style is a grandly eloquent variety of steno-language. The first sentence of the book reads, "When . . . Milton states that his argument is 'to assert Eternal Providence / And justifie the wayes of God to men' (I, 25–26), he is insisting on the rationality of his subject." A few sentences later Burden adds, "The poem is thus an exercise in clarification, finding a system and order in what could, if wrongly taken, appear to be random and inexplicable."⁴ Burden apparently sees a *Paradise Lost* that is a natural extention of Enlightenment thought, a theodicy in poetic regalia which, like the Enlightenment itself, might fairly be described as "fearful of all irrationalism," one which reduces "the meaning of holiness to the grandeur of the first cause of the universe and of morality."⁵ Milton's mission, as far as Burden understands it, is one of "saving" the Bible "from apparent arbitrariness and absurdity."⁶

The very vocabulary Burden uses gives away his hostility to any notion that *Paradise Lost* might be something more than a reasoned argument in verse. His attention fixes on the "rationality," "clarification," "system," and "order" that he sees everywhere in that poem. His Milton is the Bible's *miglior fabbro*, a kind of supreme editor who blue-pencils the Scriptures of all that is "random and inexplicable" and thereby "saves" the biblical God from His otherwise inherent "arbitrariness and absurdity." To put the case bluntly, Burden sees a Milton who successfully eliminates from *Paradise Lost* the very essential ingredients of a functioning God-talk. Burden's *Paradise Lost* is a "steno-epic." The potential sources of religious wonder and mystery, he would have us believe, Milton purged in a relentless pursuit of the logical epic.

Other critics equally committed to the principle of a logical epic find the rationality and coherence of the poem less tidy. H.R. Swardson, for one, examines its consistency and finds that

> the statements and effects in the poem have no single embracing
> context. There are, rather, separate insular contexts, each in an
> unresolved antagonism with the other. To respond to the one
> we must ignore the other.[7]

The accuracy of Swardson's assessment and his obliviousness to its
religious significance is an illustration of literary criticism's potential blind
spot when it comes to interpreting religious writing. If he finds "separate
insular contexts" in *Paradise Lost* with "no single embracing context," is it
not possible — even probable — that the kind of organizing unity he
expects to find (and does not) was not the organizing unity Milton
originally intended? I agree wholeheartedly that from Swardson's point of
view *Paradise Lost* is anything but a logical epic. I only suggest that there
are other kinds of logic capable of providing literary coherence than the
rigorously rationalistic one he exclusively honors. What Swardson
condemns on the basis of apparent inconsistency with the internal
decorum of the epic we should applaud for quite different reasons.
Swardson's "inconsistencies" are in fact our assurance that a vital, healthy
God-talk enlivens *Paradise Lost*.

Asserting the effectiveness of God-talk in *Paradise Lost* does not
deny the poem's patent rational structure and detail, however. The
complaint that should be made against Burden, Swardson and others of
their persuasion is not that what they say about the epic is wrong, but
that in being so adamantly half-right their comments lock *Paradise Lost*
into an interpretive context (language game, if you will) which renders
serious inquiry into what the epic might be trying to accomplish
religiously irrelevant. Burden and Swardson are cousins to the Sceptic in
Wisdom's parable of the invisible gardener. They impose a language game
on the epic which effectively excludes consideration of its religious
conduct, for it is a language game that constitutionally refuses to
acknowledge that such a thing as God-talk exists.

A better language game within which to talk about *Paradise Lost*
would be one which permits us to question seriously the propriety of
demanding a "single embracing context" (as Swardson means that phrase)
in a work which professes to be both religious in style and content. The
point is that the language of faith (God-talk) is frozen out of a context that
is so rationalistically secured that no tolerance remains for the
characteristic logical improprieties that enliven it. God-talk, in other
words, rarely subsists in the kind of "single embracing context" that
Swardson describes. It gets its coherence, as Auerbach tells us, *vertically*
from God instead of *horizontally* from its "fit" with the other empirical

constituents of its milieu.[8] Where "horizontal logic" sees "separate insular contexts," "vertical logic" sees a "single embracing context," and, of course, vice-versa. To insist that the communication of religious knowledge conform consistently to the dictates of horizontal logic is not only to reduce its impact and significance to human scale, but to engage in the presumptuous circularity of the argument that declares the universe rational on grounds that if it were irrational it would not meet the demands of reason.

Horizontal *and* vertical logics are at work in *Paradise Lost;* Milton was rational *and more* when he created the poem. He saw the development of a theodicy as only part of his task, and he was at least equally concerned about including conditions for genuine religious insight. This means that the "separate insular contexts" to which Swardson objects ought not to be condemned nor even explained into unity. They should be understood instead as legitimate features of the manifold logic of God-talk through which *Paradise Lost* makes its compromise with reason and thus genuinely and appropriately becomes "fraught with background."

Let us try to meet the challenge of the "logical epic" head on. Swardson is perhaps a better adversary than Burden (or Waldock or John Peter, to name a few other likely candidates) because of the deliberately hostile stance he assumes toward *Paradise Lost* and because of the concise clarity with which he isolates his objections. In answering to Swardson, we answer to the critical persuasion he represents at large.

Swardson begins with a familiar critical issue. He notes a "fundamental strain, or tension" which he feels "originates in a conflict between the literary and the religious requirements Milton faced in the kind of poem he proposed."[9] He contends that the formal requirements of the epic pull against the requirements of Christian belief and, by way of example, he offers Milton's description of Mammon in Book One:

> *Mammon* led them on,
> *Mammon,* the least erected Spirit that fell
> From Heav'n, for ev'n in heav'n his looks and thoughts
> Were always downward bent, admiring more
> The riches of Heav'n's pavement, trodd'n Gold,
> Then aught divine or holy else enjoy'd
> In vision beatific . . . (I, 678–84)

Swardson admits the *dramatic* success of this description. Its psychological realism promotes realistic action in the narrative. But despite its powerful "local effect," Swardson is dismayed by "what it implies about Heaven." Here are some of the questions that disturb him: "How can Mammon as an unfallen spirit show these signs of avarice? Can we picture him as one of the blessed admiring the streets of gold for their wealth? . . . Isn't this a sin before Sin had entered the universe? . . . What, furthermore, can gold or wealth mean to unfallen Mammon in such a situation?" And finally, is it not a "terrible reduction of heavenly existence to picture one so high in spiritual excellence bent over musing on the worth of Heaven's pavement?"[10]

To frame a rebuttal to these questions is a challenging obligation, for they appear responsibly conceived, logical, apparently damaging to the theological integrity of the epic, and quite vexing because they seem to belie the sheer uncomplicated delight the passage usually inspires on first reading. In the face of them, we may feel a little like the Believer in Wisdom's parable, who stands unconvinced but helpless before the empirical evidence against his position that the Sceptic dredges up. Were we to follow the Believer, we would probably succumb to the Sceptic's language game by retorting with several counter-arguments on the Sceptic's own terms. For example, must we take the admittedly "loaded" moral terms "least erected," "downward bent," "admiring more / The riches of Heav'n's pavement" necessarily as "signs of avarice"? Could not "least erected" serve as a kind of determinative phrase which sets the context for what follows? If so, can we not then see the remarks as hierarchical rather than moral judgments? As Milton points out over and over again, there are *degrees* of angelic status even in prelapsarian innocence, degrees which apparently work independently of moral categories which occur subsequent to a fall. The "least erected" angel, Mammon, is an unfallen angel of the lowest degree *not* on the basis of any avarice attached to his character, but on the basis perhaps of his *potentiality* for avarice. A similar argument is often used to justify the hints of vanity which appear in Milton's unfallen Eve. The point is that vulnerability to avaricious temptation is a personality trait rather than the moral status of Mammon at this point, a distinction which John Donne, for one, was fond of making in reference to regenerate sinners:

> A covetous person, who is now truly converted to God, he will exercise a spiritual covetousness still . . . So will a voluptuous man, who is turned to God, find plenty and deliciousness enough in him, to feed his soul.[11]

Finally, we might point out that it is questionable whether the admiration of Heaven's riches can be called "a sin before Sin had entered the universe," for the simple reason that admiration of riches became a sin only subsequent to the fall. Besides, Swardson's objection seems to be based upon the dubious notion of sin as a kind of substantial commodity that enters the universe at a certain time — that it is not and has not always been imminent. This seems a misleading distortion of the Christian dogma of sin as *actus purus*, for the purpose, presumably, of maintaining allegorical consistency at the expense of Christian insight.

Having argued in this way, however, what have we accomplished? By replying to Swardson on his own rational terms have we not undermined the premise that there is a God-talk operative in *Paradise Lost* which is obedient to a logical structure all its own? To prove logical consistency in the passage through compiling debater's points seems a rather dry and humorless activity hardly appropriate to a passage that itself contains such a rare instance of Miltonic humor. A better point to begin on may be the quality of our initial response, and this quality is clearly determined by the attitude we bring to the passage as we read.

Swardson's attitude is that of the "serious" reader. "All I mean by 'reading seriously' is that we try to believe what he [Milton] says," he explains.

> We attend to what the words mean because we want to under-
> stand what Milton means. But it is just by attending to what the
> words mean in their full and normal senses that we are thrown
> into confusion. I think that if this goes on long enough we be-
> come fatigued at the effort and decide, perhaps subconsciously,
> just to share Milton's irresponsibility toward language.[12]

Swardson's explanation of the "serious reader" comes as close to defining steno-reading as is possible and, consequently, flies in the face of Wittgenstein's principle (upon which our account of God-talk is based) that the meaning of a word is determined by its *use*. It is inevitable that he should take as "picture" models (the Mammon episode, for example) what Milton intended to be disclosure models.[13] Instead of looking *through* the Mammon passage toward the religious discernment it was designed to arouse, Swardson looks *at* it and commits the semantic idolatry of mistaking the means for the end.

Steno-reading passages like the Mammon description in *Paradise Lost* will unquestionably lead to precisely the conclusion Swardson ultimately arrives at: that the epic, "with its gulf between the official ethical lesson and the actual ethical atmosphere, is really the greatest children's poem ever written."[14] The more religiously sophisticated approach — one we can reasonably assume that Milton's original readers took — is to acknowledge that the structure of the Mammon description (and the many models similar to it in *Paradise Lost)* is the structure of the parable. When the many "separate, insular contexts" of *Paradise Lost* are read as parables rather than, say, scenes, episodes, or even alegories,[15] a great deal, if not all, of the "fundamental strain, or tension" that otherwise attends is relieved.

The fundamental Christian employment of the parable, we recall, is to effect an interpenetration of divine and worldly realities. Like all effective forms of God-talk, the parable is open to both horizontal and vertical (secular and sacred) logics. It is rooted in realistically empirical soil, but it always bears with it theological qualification which more often than not appears as logical impropriety. Robert Funk, for instance, says that

> like the cleverly distorted picture puzzles children used to work, the parable is a picture puzzle which prompts the question, What's wrong with this picture? Distortions of everydayness, exaggerated realism, distended concreteness, incompatible elements often subtly drawn — are what prohibit the parable from coming to us in the literal sense.[16]

As a matter of fact, it is the parable's *resistance* to literal interpretation that gives it its unique character.

If it is true that the Mammon passage functions parabolically, Swardson's reading, which we might account as a "rationalizing of its meaning" that patently *does* "tend to destroy its power as image," must be judged counter to the epic's religious intention at this point, a simple case of Swardson's missing the point. Our obligation, then, is to examine the passage to see what specific features of the parable it possesses in order to ascertain whether or not we are justified in urging that a parabolic, as opposed to a "steno-", reading of Mammon's description is the more appropriate to Milton's intention.

Dodd, we recall, isolated four specific characteristics of the parable: it is figurative, it possesses natural realism, it has an arresting vividness or strangeness, and it never allows itself to petrify into a single didactic moral. Swardson's argument concedes outright several of these parabolic features in the Mammon passage. As a matter of fact, his major complaint is that Mammon is drawn entirely too realistically to avoid conflict with his relative perfection as an angel. Implied in Swardson's objection, of course, is that Milton's Mammon is either a simile or metaphor, drawn in human terms, for the "real" Mammon whose purity is sullied by the human model Milton imposes on him. And yet Swardson, when it suits him, appears to ignore that Mammon's human "realism" is a metaphor. He seems to speak as though there were in fact two Mammons, a human and an angelic, both of them stumbling in and out of their appropriate language games, here to do violence to Christian dogma and there to disrupt the "single embracing context" allegedly constituting the epic's internal decorum. No wonder, then, that what a parabolic reading of the passage would see as its "vividness or strangeness" Swardson dismisses as the consequences of a fundamental incompatibility between Christian principle and epic convention.

A horizontal logician abhors strangeness because it has no place in his system; the vertical logician covets it because the system that governs him lies outside his understanding and he is always eager for new disclosures. For the one, strangeness is inconsistency; for the other, it is insight. Swardson, it appears, is committed to a horizontal logic. The vividness or strangeness of the Mammon passage is for him its incompatibility with common sense. The pieces simply refuse to fall into place, and "strangeness" inevitably becomes synonymous with "mistake." Others may find the passage hermeneutically fertile. The rush of provocative questions that the passage spawns, each one bearing its own fresh cargo of articulation possibilities, are full of potential religious disclosure: How odd that Mammon, "the least erected Spirit," should be a "leader." And the humorous wordplay with "least erected" and "downward bent." What a provocatively ambivalent blend of words denoting both status and physical description. Mammon, of course, is "least erected" both actually and figuratively, but he is perhaps more significantly "bent" physically over to admire the golden pavements at the same time that such an activity is his "bent." Even the word "riches" takes on an irony from context; to think that "riches" in heaven are what the divine denizens "trod" upon provides a richly ironic value judgment. The point is that the passage is literally alive with hermeneutical and even logological activity which the "logical" point of view simply ignores or, worse, cites as Milton's "irresponsibility toward language."[17] Mammon's description is indeed "vivid or strange" in the parabolic sense of those words, and it is this very quality which affords it a religiously salutary purposefulness.

Finally, what kind of applications does the Mammon passage recommend? No specific ones on the face of it, but it is suggestive of an attitude that emerges from the logical oddities, the puns and the paradoxes that make up the very fabric of the description. We have, for example, all the necessary raw material for developing a Christian colloquy on riches or even a reconfirmation of the entire Christian value system. The passage also teases us with the mystery of sin (How does it occur? When does it occur? Is sin inevitable? What constitutes the committing of a sin?). But most important of all, the passage applies itself to us viscerally by forcing Mammon upon our very personalities. We become Mammon through a deliberately designed identification process. Here is this angelic abstraction, laden with its impressive cargo of symbolic significance, suddenly incarnated before our eyes, and immediately the frailty of *that* flesh we see as the frailty of *our* flesh. Mammon is "arrestingly vivid" because we see ourselves in him; he is "strange" because he is simultaneously an angel caught up in the awesome drama of heavenly apostasy. Suddenly it must occur to us that the great cosmological drama of divine treason which Mammon "leads" is the identical drama that is reenacted daily in the individual Christian's soul. Mammon brings two worlds together; the homely and the cosmic meld. His predicament is discovered as our predicament, and we are stricken with the realization that it is not we who are interpreting Mammon but Mammon who is interpreting us.

Swardson's reading of the Mammon passage differs from a parabolic reading primarily in that he tends to see the elements of the segment as ends in themselves, as constituents of a narrative rather than *means* to religious ends beyond. As parable, however, the passage can be seen as a qualified model situation — an attempt to arrange admittedly empirical detail in such a way as to create a situation capable of evoking religious discernments unattainable through discursive means. To be sure, the parabolic mode of expression necessarily forfeits the logical uniformity of the epic's "single embracing context," but it does so in order that a dimension of religious depth might develop within the chinks and fault lines of the rational structure. The "separate insular contexts" of *Paradise Lost* are the *sine qua non* of its religious vitality; again, they cause the epic to be "fraught with background."

The major burden of Swardson's argument that a tension exists between the conflicting demands of Christianity and epic convention falls on his objection to what he calls the "whole martial atmosphere in the poem."[18] He feels that Milton "is concerned to emphasize the martial atmosphere even where his Christian fable does not require it." There is certainly a great deal of evidence to back this claim; the poem is full of "heroic warriors," "warlike machinery and technical military terms at every opportunity," just as Swardson says, and Murray Roston points out that although "during the Middle Ages and Renaissance, the incident remained no more than a brief precursor to the central story of the fall in Eden, a momentary act of defiance punished immediately by Satan's expulsion from heaven . . . . In Milton's *Paradise Lost* the War in Heaven occupies not a few lines but an entire book."[19] A typical example, which Swardson cites, is the following description of Heaven in Book Two:

> the Towr's of Heav'n are fill'd
> With Armed watch, that render all access
> Impregnable; oft on the bordering Deep
> Encamp thir Legions, or with obscure wing
> Scout far and wide into the Realm of night,
> Scorning surprise. (II, 129–34)

In addition to the fact that we find this kind of latent bellicosity in Heaven in scenes that occur even before the rebellion, Swardson objects that "it is counter to the logic that Omniscience could be surprised. The Christian God cannot be surprised. To suggest that he *can* be not only violates the logic demanded by theology but it goes against the instincts given us in the usual Christian training."

Our defense of Milton here is predictable. We must charge Swardson with pursuing a doggedly literal reading of what is really a highly charged parabolic situation. God is not *really* capable of being surprised; He does not *really* need watchtowers or advance scouts. Milton merely exploits military models to help us appreciate Heaven's exclusivity for the righteous. Evildoers simply do not *sneak* in. To assume the physical reality of armed towers in Heaven or even a figurative need for them is tantamount to asking to inspect the Salvation Army's howitzers. Milton was after much greater hermeneutical game in this passage than mere acquiescence to the formal demands of the epic.

Nevertheless, Swardson's point deserves better than that. Our defense of the "whole martial atmosphere in the poem" really rests on the general propriety of military images as models to the primary theme of the entire epic. It was not the formal demands of the epic that primarily caused Milton's sabre-rattling throughout *Paradise Lost,* although epic convention certainly provided added incentive; it was the fact that his story, both religiously and narratively conceived, is about the greatest adversary situation ever: rebellion against God. The religious logic that pervades the poem down to the bedrock of its linguistic structure is that you are either *with* God or *against* Him. The most fundamental assertion that Christianity makes about sin is that it is treason. Satan is the "Adversary"; Mammon turns his back on God; we fallen readers are His enemies because we violate His will. What more appropriate set of models could there be with which to impress Christians with their status in the Christian cosmological scheme of things than models of warfare? The fact that Swardson himself says Milton plays the martial scenes "always for suspense, horror, awe, portentiousness"[20] only encourages us that they indeed are powerfully hermeneutical tools as Milton uses them.

What about the notorious war in Heaven itself? Here is a "separate, insular context" that exhibits so much vivid strangeness that interpretive response to it has itself taken on a strangely vivid inconsistency. The spectrum of critical displeasure regarding the War in Heaven is all too familiar. Voltaire begins the litany by protesting the "visible Contradiction which reigns in that Episode," referring, of course, to the absurd pointlessness of a battle in which an Omnipotent God can order the expulsion of inferior opponents while still encouraging the fiction that "the Battle hangs doubtful."[21] Dr. Johnson disapproves strongly of the "confusion of spirit and matter" in the work, the "absurdity of presenting immaterial and immortal spirits as engaged in physical warfare."[22] Taine takes the position of an exasperated spectator: "Was it worthwhile leaving earth to find in heaven carriage-words, buildings, artillery, a manual of tactics?"[23] John Peter, sharing some of Taine's dismay, wonders "what all the fuss has been about" after considering that the battle is "reported with such fidelity and at such length."[24] Broadbent maintains that, since any attempt to depict the war seriously was hopeless from the start, Milton ought to have abandoned all effort to portray it in terrestrial terms and simply to have ". . . treated it all as science fiction." He is troubled by the heroic epic conventions in the scene which, he says, "accumulate so wearisomely that they overwhelm their own point. Instead of consigning war to romantic epicism they back-fire as self-parody."[25]

James A. Freeman suggests, from the standpoint of martial history, that concern about the propriety of the War may be only a modern preoccupation. "The double goal of *Paradise Lost* — to captivate a learned audience and to correct its attitude — springs," he argues, "from one fact Milton knew about his contemporaries: almost everybody approved of war . . . . In order to lure others from the road to destruction, Milton had to prove that he knew more about the ideas he attacked than experts who sponsored them."[26]

Arnold Stein's lively and plausible defense starts a trend which accepts the absurdity of the War in Heaven as deliberate: the War is "a kind of diabolical scherzo, like some of Beethoven's — with more than human laughter, too elevated, and comprehensive, and reverberating, not to be terribly funny."[27] His account proved very convincing to subsequent readers, but engaging and fun as it is to tap the war's farcical potential, not everyone joins the party. Roston, for one, writes that "read in isolation, [Stein's] essay is impressive and persuasive. The trouble arises as one turns back to the poem in order to apply this comic reading to the text: for the humour simply is not there."[28] For Roston, the war is a "solemnly conceived scene of immense vigour and turmoil, a baroque clash of forces as Rubens would have delighted to paint." He adds:

> Taken out of its baroque context and scrutinised in a coldly logical light, the idea of ethereal spirits donning armour is indeed ridiculous . . . . Like the great religious artists of the baroque, Milton's purpose is to go beyond the factual world and to provide for the willing spectator a vision of superhuman forces in tumultuous yet physically realised conflict, so that out of that compression of energy will erupt the imaginative release into the infinite, the upward surge of religious faith.[29]

Joseph Summers sees both the ridiculous and the sublime in the War; ". . . this battle is both above and below our expectations,"[30] he contends, and from the point of view of God-talk his words perhaps say more than they know, for like the parable, this scene both disarms us with its naive epic heroism at the same time its vividly comic strangeness teases us, as I hope to show, into active thought and unexpected religious discernment. Summers, at any rate, concludes that the War is a kind of learning experience for Satan, the fallen and unfallen angels, Adam and Eve, and the reader. "All," he says, "have learned . . . the inevitable results of 'warfare' against the Almighty and His Messiah": that "to oppose the universe by our wills or our technology, as to oppose the good, is not heroic but absurd."[31]

Stanley Fish proposes a similar defense. Responding to John Peter's "What is all the fuss about?" he replies,

> . . . the battle is "reportd with such fidelity and at such length" in order to allow the reader time to construct from its thrusts and parries a working definition of heroism and to extend it by analogy to the crisis of the Fall . . . . In addition, he is encouraged to see in the battle an image of the struggle he himself engages in daily. The correspondences between the military situation as it exists in Book VI and the concept of spiritual warfare are easily established . . . .

The principal correspondence, Fish says, is that "in both contexts, there is a divine imperative, 'be ye perfect', 'drive out the rebels', which is beyond the individual's unaided capabilities." This imperative involves one in "a series of indeterminate actions" which "often *appear* ridiculous and base" (the apparent indignities that Christians are called upon to suffer for their faith). Heroism, Fish explains, consists of continuing in spite of the humiliations or, "more properly, because of them; and this continuing is an affirmation of faith in a deity who judges intent and does not ultimately require more than can be performed."[32]

What we have then is a long record of indecisiveness about the propriety and the purpose of Book Six. There appears to be, as Voltaire originally noted, some basic contradiction in the episode which generates a rather stimulating variety of complaints and defenses: the war, of course, is narratively illogical; it displays a bewildering "confusion of spirit and matter"; its "custard pie" cachet threatens the epic's sublimity. On the other hand, perhaps the conventions of baroque art defend Milton's procedures here; perhaps the militaristic enthusiasms of his contemporaries required a satiric correction which the depiction of the War provided; perhaps we ought not regard the scene with such narrative literalism and instead appreciate what its admittedly bizarre features tell us about heroism, disobedience, humility and war itself. Perhaps, but the most interesting insight into the War in Heaven is William Madsen's eschatalogical reading. "The purpose of Raphael's narrative is not merely to demonstrate to Adam the consequences of disobedience," he says,

> Nor is its purpose to reveal that there is a Platonic idea of War
> in Heaven, of which mere earthly wars are an imperfect
> embodiment. Milton . . . is not really interested in the parti-
> culars . . . of Satan's first battle with God. What he is interested
> in, and what he wants his readers to be interested in, is
> Raphael's *account* of that war, which is a different matter.
> Raphael's account is not moral allegory, nor is it primarily a
> metaphorical description of what happened a long time ago in
> Heaven. It is a shadow of things to come, and more particularly
> it is a shadow of this last age of the world and of the Second
> Coming of Christ.[33]

Madsen is interested to place the narrative of the War in Heaven in a
typological setting, and in the process of doing so he strives to define it
formally through an insightful process of remotion: it is *not* an allegory,
not a metaphorical description of divine history, and *not even an
accommodation*, for in a footnote he says,

> It is, of course, simply a fiction that Raphael is "measuring
> things in Heav'n by things on Earth" (VI.893), and it is absurd
> to claim that Milton here actually employs the method of
> accommodation. Because of the impossibility of looking behind
> the narrative to the actual conflict in Heaven (whatever its
> nature, about which Milton had no more special knowledge
> than anyone else) I have regarded its significance as primarily,
> though not exclusively, typological, that is, oriented toward
> the future.[34]

Typological it unquestionably is, but typology is itself merely one facet of
the manifold logic of God-talk, and I believe Madsen's most valuable
service in this passage is to extricate Raphael's narrative from the
misleading narrow confines of the so-called doctrine of accommodation
which, like some other literary red herrings, has cut off our appreciation
of its full hermeneutical potential.

   Dr. Johnson, as usual, struck at the heart of the literary problem of
the War by objecting that "the confusion of spirit and matter which
pervades the whole narration of the war in heaven fills it with
incongruity." Like Swardson, he was worried about the consistency of the
poem's internal decorum, which is violated when such scandalous
improprieties as angelic pain and bleeding blur the natural distinctions
between the sacred and the profane. Despite the fact that biblical
language (the standard of all God-talk) revels in such insightful
confusions, Johnson seems to prefer literary decorum over religious
impropriety and therefore forfeits much of the poem's evocative
potential.

   No, the religious reading of Raphael's account is not at all disturbed by the mixture of spirit and matter that so troubled Dr. Johnson and (in more subtle but no less real ways) most subsequent literary critics. Quite to the contrary, it accurately recognizes the familiar incarnational mode of a well-functioning God-talk and eagerly anticipates its revelatory possibilities. For there to be religious fecundity in the narration, matter and spirit *must* fraternize. The more riotously the better. Ian Ramsey, in his account of religious language, identifies its essential character as logical impropriety, noting that the earliest evangelists met the challenge of expressing the uniqueness of Christianity by "taking as many traditional phrases as they could, and mixing them in the most riotous manner possible." He points to a series of logically mixed speeches of St. Peter in Acts: "God hath made him *both Lord* and *Christ*, this Jesus whom ye crucified" (Acts 2:36), and "Jesus whom ye slew, hanging him on a tree . . . him did God exalt with his right hand to be *a Prince* and *a Saviour* for to give repentance to Israel, and remission of sins" (Acts 5:30, 31). "What a riotous mixture of phrases this is," says Ramsey,

> belonging intrinsically to so many different logical areas with a diversity even greater than that of the Old Testament. This riotous mixing is in effect a rough and ready attempt to secure that special logical impropriety needed to express the Christian message. Each word is logically qualified by the presence of the others, and in this way each word comes to display a suitable measure of impropriety.[35]

Ramsey speaks of biblical phrases, but the ability of logical impropriety to provoke religious discernment is a feature God-talk exploits in virtually all of its forms, even epic narrative. That Raphael should employ the manifold logic of God-talk in his attempts to arouse discernment in Adam and Eve should not be surprising, and I think the various literary complaints about his account of the War (its improper mixture of spirit and matter, the logical futility of a pointless war, the improper mingling of farce and tragedy, the general confusion of sacred and profane elements) bear witness to the authenticity of his God-talk. Madsen is right. Raphael does not "accommodate" divine history for Adam and Eve, he merely enunciates it in its proper idiom — God-talk.

Ebeling, too, casts light on what is happening religiously in the War in Heaven by reminding us that

> the language of faith . . . exists only in an encounter with the confusion of languages in the world. To extricate itself from this encounter would bring it only an apparent security . . . . If the language of faith draws apart from the world and consequently becomes deformed in itself, it deserves to be abandoned completely to the world.[36]

The hermeneutical poverty of a language divorced from the world perhaps explains why Milton's Raphael claims he is "accommodating" the hexameral events when in fact he follows Moses' *literal* account of the Creation. By conceding that he is "measuring things in Heav'n by things on Earth" (VI, 893), Raphael simultaneously emphasizes the "otherness" of transcendent heaven from the world and also supplies the means through which the double vision essential to an effective God-talk can deepen his account. Tasso felt that Christian poets should "avoid sacred histories, for difficult problems of feigning arise if a poet tries to deal with them, and without feigning he is simply a historian."[37] Of necessity, it would seem Raphael "feigns," but for the best of reasons; sacred history demands a sacred idiom which, by its very nature, requires an incarnational measurement of "things in Heav'n by things on Earth."

If one were searching for a model which, when theologically qualified, might serve well to support the logic of encounter, what has more empirical anchorage, more discernment potential, more dynamic, performative activity than war itself? It would be hard to imagine a more fertile terrain than the battlefield for this mode of God-talk to perform at its best. General Booth certainly seemed to have understood this when he named his organization the Salvation Army, and Ebeling's observation that the language of faith lives *only* when it is in contention with the language of the world suggests how and why a conflict between sacred and profane combatants might be expected to throw off an abundance of hermeneutical sparks. It might also suggest to readers of Book Six where their attention should center—not on the "worldly" impedimental of Satan's army (which, with its very human pain, "blood," and technological ingenuity, provides God-talk's requisite empirical anchorage), and not on the righteous innocence of the divine forces whose position is emphatically enunciated by Abdiel's language of faith, but on the dynamic, logically "improper," contention between them. The War, in other words, is a visually rendered collision of opposing "logical styles" of the sort exploited by Herbert in "The Collar," by the language of Scripture, and by Milton consistently throughout *Paradise Lost*.

The logic of encounter, we recall, does not create contests in order to produce winners, for its mode is not to demonstrate the superiority of one point of view over another but to superintend the ignition of the hermeneutical sparks that result from their collision. Max Black's term "interaction metaphor," referring to the way one analogue acts as a lens through which to see the other, captures the incarnational spirit of the process well. Unlike most analogies, this sort does not supplant one of the analogues with another, but maintains them both in kinetic interaction. To detect such interaction in a text, we search for contentious juxtapositions of the sort that abound in Raphael's narration of the War in Heaven.

We might notice, for example, how Milton's God insists on a curious parity between the angelic combatants, sending Michael and Gabriel off to battle with troops "Equal in number to that godless crew / Rebellious" (VI, 49–50). Not only is there a quantitative parity, but, from the heroically flattering description of Satan dressed for battle, we sense a deliberately bestowed qualitative one as well:

> High in the midst exalted as a god
> Th' Apostate in his sun-bright chariot sat
> Idol of majesty divine, enclosed
> With flaming Cherubim, and golden shields;
> Then lighted from his gorgeous throne (VI, 99–103)

Satan is portrayed as regally in his element, and only the qualification supplied by the word "Idol" shadows its comparison with the depiction of "The chariot of the Paternal Deity" (VI, 750) that Milton gives us later in the Book. *Not* in their element are Satan's opponents. Raphael comments how

> strange to us it seemed
> At first, that angel should with angel war,
> And in fierce hosting meet, who wont to meet
> So oft in festivals of joy and love
> Unanimous, as sons of one great Sire (VI, 91–95)

War and the bearing of military arms are alien to the innocence of angelic experience. The uncorrupted angels are deliberately made to seem uncomfortable with weapons. When Satan's artillery places them "A while in trouble" (VI, 634), they throw away their arms (VI, 639) as though they were impediments rather than aids to victory. Why does God, who has clearly ordained and orchestrated the War even before it begins (VI, 689–703), insist that his contention with Satan be played out on Satan's terms, that is, in *military* combat? One might almost assume that God conducts the war for its own sake. He exceeds the requirements of fair play by limiting the quantity of the heavenly troops to match Satan's; He affords Satan full military pomp and circumstance; He allows the battle to proceed, knowing all along that conditions assure victory for neither side. God appears to engineer a deliberate military stalemate.

What purpose can this serve? Narratively, the suspenseless stalemate is pointless, as so many critics lamentingly point out. But a war depicted for war's own sake *does* discourage taking sides and frees our attention from partisanship so that it can savor the dynamics of the sheer conflict itself. Not the outcome, but the *situation* becomes the center of the reader's concern. He begins to see how Satan's fallen militancy serves as a lens through which to see divine love and wrath, and how divine love becomes a lens through which to reassess the familiar epic virtues of heroism, puissance, courage, pride, fame and glory. Glory, in fact, stands as a cameo illustration of how the logic of encounter generates what Kenneth Burke might deem a logological interaction. Satan, in responding to Michael's scolding, acknowledges the logological transformation of "glory": "Err not that so shall end / The strife which thou call'st evil, but we style / The strife of glory" (VI, 288–290). Glory, for Satan, is a consequence of successful conflict. The full effect of the transformation is suspended until the end of the Book when Christ responds to God:

> 'O Father, O Supreme of heav'nly Thrones,
> First, highest, holiest, best, thou always seek'st
> To glorify thy Son, I always thee,
> As is most just; this I my glory account,
> My exaltation, and my whole delight.' (VI, 723–727)

Sacred and profane "glories" collide, prompting the reader to consider the source of true glory. The interplay between the two connotations of "glory" is the hermeneutical yield, and the same can be said for a number of other logological pairings. Take "arms," for example. We have already seen how to the good angels military arms prove almost vestigial, even an encumbrance, suggesting that, like the divinely legislated parity of the combatants, they are a concession to Satan rather than genuinely helpful weapons. The sword of Michael comes rather pointedly from "the armory of God" (VI, 321), but that it proves the instrument by which "Satan first knew pain" (VI, 327) shows how it serves as a metaphorical transition, rather than a literal weapon, pointing toward the "arms" Christ puts out from God's armory at the end of the Book:

> But whom thou hat'st, I hate, and can put on
> Thy terrors, as I put thy mildness on,
> Image of thee in all things; and shall soon,
> Armed with thy might, rid heav'n of these rebelled (VI, 733–737)

The transformation provides a short lesson in sacred and profane weaponry.

The equally-matched, unwinnable war, which God arranges by "overruling" and "limiting" (VI, 228–229) the contending forces, makes no sense to conventional literary logic, but appreciated as God-talk it spawns endless illuminating juxtapositions which, like parables, "tease the mind into active thought." One way to sound the hermeneutical possibilities is through onlook analysis which, as we have seen, provides the means through which we can assess the performative force of the manifold encounters in the war, that is, their efficiency in affecting attitudes.

Through the model of war, Milton's Raphael treats Adam and the "fit audience" to a series of onlook collisions. Satan's onlooks, which generally provide the requisite empirical anchorage upon which the ultimate religious discernments spring, parallel those sponsored by epic conventions, and Milton is at pains to make them deliberately attractive. Satan is physically heroic and he displays impeccable epic virtues: courage, valor, magisterial pride, sharp intellect and an acutely satiric sense of humor. Although Abdiel is available to remind us that Satan is only a "resemblance of the Highest" (VI, 114), that resemblance is attractively close and appealing. Satan "looks on" war as an epic hero would. His conventional epic scorn for the "turncoat" Abdiel even affords Milton some gratuitous logological opportunities with such charged words as "seditious angel" (VI, 152), "merited reward" (VI, 153), and even "synod" (VI, 156) — words usually found on divine tongues — establishing the scene as a parody of his own apostasy. The much criticized "punning" in the War comes exclusively from Satan's lips and does not seem to me, at least, any less appropriate than traditional epic boasting or the ironic litotes of Beowulf's speeches. The point is that Satan's onlooks in Book VI self-consciously accumulate into a model of heroic ideals which is subjected to a variety of direct and indirect theological qualification. Satan looks on military strife as "glory," puissance as "arms," fame as "the praise of men" (VI, 376), and perhaps most significantly, truth as that which experience confirms. His pain and bleeding at the hands of Michael's sword do not induce an appropriate humility but instead nourish the false comfort of an apparently invincible self-reliance.

> True is, less firmly armed,
> Some disadvantage we endured and pain,
> Till now not known, but known as soon contemned,
> Since now we find this our empyreal form
> Incapable of mortal injury
> Imperishable, and though pierced with wound,
> Soon closing, and by native vigor healed. (VI, 428–436)

These onlooks eventually confront the rival onlooks of Christ expressed at the end of the Book. The effect is not that Christ's onlooks *trump* those of Satan (although to a genuine Christian sensibility they of course do), but that they interact dynamically providing mutual illumination and assuring God-talk its incarnational character.

Up to this point we have been regarding the hermeneutical effect of the military stalemate prior to the intervention of Christ, but that intervention is no mere introduction of fresh reinforcements; it is a qualitative alteration of the context. Just as God's creation of the Heavens and the Earth is logically distinct from Christopher Wren's creation of St.

Paul's, so Christ's "victory" over Satan's army is logically different from Wellington's success at Waterloo. Christ's divine "victory" is the theological qualification of war itself in the largest sense. The most extravagantly conceived capabilities of military conflict (including cannons and hurled mountains) are ineffectual to resolve ultimate issues. Such resolutions are effected only through Christ. God's words make this explicit:

> Two days are therefore passed, the third is thine;
> For thee I have ordained it, and thus far
> Have suffered, that the glory may be thine
> Of ending this great war, since none but thou
> Can end it. (VI, 699–703)

The intervention of Christ thus generates an almost endless series of onlooks: I look on Christ as the conquerer of war, as the neutralizer of divine wrath, as the restorer or order, as the end of true glory, as the ultimate weapon, as the conqueror of Satan, as the enemy of apostasy, as the Word of the New Testament demonstrating the alternative to vengeance, showing the way, the truth and the light. The deliberately arranged encounter between divine love and worldly conflict produces an incarnational God-talk at its most effective, impressing us with no uncertainty that War is indeed Hell.

8

The Logic of Encounter

> ". . . the language of faith never ceases to exist in
> the form of an encounter in the midst of the con-
> fusion of the languages present in the world."
> — Gerhard Ebeling[1]

In the last chapter we discussed the War in Heaven as a "visual"
embodiment of the logic of encounter, making the point that just as the
collision of rival language games can often throw off hermeneutical
sparks, so too can battles ignite religious insight when readers transcend
mere partisan involvement and appreciate the conflict as a performative
model. The problem with this point of view (as with so many others
towards *Paradise Lost*) is that it seems to place unusual interpretive
obligations upon its audience. Few readers are scolded as regularly as
those of *Paradise Lost*, for inattentiveness and irresponsibility, and it
seems only fair to ask why *should* they be expected to assume such a
religiously sophisticated stance toward the epic as we seem to be
demanding? A predictable response, of course, might be that the
seventeenth-century "fit audience" simply *was* more religiously
sophisticated than today's profane reader, but surely a Christian author
like Milton, responsible to the evangelical claims we assume he felt, and
beholden too to the unconscious logical pressures of God-talk, can be
expected to have embedded more overt encouragement for such a
performative reading of his poem than mere confidence in the like-
mindedness of his audience. I think we can, and I think Milton did.

The embedded encouragement I have in mind is the running debate
between Abdiel and Satan which prefaces and, in a sense, suffuses the
battle. It is a debate which, like the battle itself, involves not simply the
conflict of two points of view, but the conflict of immiscible ontological
assumptions. The debate is the war's libretto, the score according to
which the performative movements of the battle are realized.

95

The very names "Abdiel" (Servant of God) and "Satan" (Adversary) anticipate a situation where a logical of encounter will flourish. Like the debators in Professor Wisdom's parable of the Invisible Gardener, each plays a language game with different rules. In a normal debate we generally judge one or the other side to be the winner on the basis of common criteria. In the Abdiel-Satan debates, however, we soon see that *two* sets of criteria are operative, both of which have considerable ethical and religious hold upon the Christian. Satan's speeches, for example, have a great deal to commend them from an ethical point of view. He argues with an egalitarian fervor indistinguishable from Milton's own in the political pamphlets. Conversely, Abdiel's speeches reflect an uncompromising commitment to divine obedience. Each position, taken independently, reflects exemplary values. It is only when they confront each other in the framework of a formal debate that their incompatibility becomes shockingly apparent and the potential religious insight within the situation is released. What in fact happens?

Clearly, Abdiel is motivated by "right" reason, which sponsors a God-talk characterized by the "logic of obedience." For him, the verification of all propositions is their consistency with God's will. Satan's "natural" reason, on the other hand, sponsors a quite different language game. For him, the verification of all propositions is their consistency with "appearances," which his apostasy is hell-bent to "save." As Wisdom's parable illustrates, such opposing language games possess only the *appearance* of mutual negotiability. In fact, there is no common ground between them. They are logically immiscible.

The empirical cast of Satan's logic is clear from the passage he delivers just before Abdiel first rises to challenge him at the meeting of the rebel angels in the North Quarter of Heaven:

> Who can in reason then or right assume
> Monarchy over such as live by right
> His equals, if in power and splendor less,
> In freedom equal? or can introduce
> Law and Edict on us, who without law
> Err not? (V, 794–799)

Satan's pose, of course, is one of dispassionate, objective inquiry, but the basis of his "objectivity" (appearances) provokes incredulous dismay in Abdiel. Satan has in effect reduced God to just another empirical item in the heavenly landscape and has rendered Him accountable to an exterior law which apparently confers "equal freedom" on *all* heavenly beings. In Satan's account, God is rendered a thing among things. Scientific scepticism is born.

To Abdiel, Satan's words make as much sense as a repeal of the

law of gravity. The commitment of his God-talk to obedience is as clear
as Satan's to appearances:

> Shalt thou give Law unto God, shalt thou dispute
> With him the points of liberty, who made
> Thee what thou art, and form'd the Pow'rs of Heav'n
> Such as he pleas'd, and circumscrib'd thir being? (V, 822–825)

The subliminal logics of both statements really contend over the issue of
what validates a truth claim: what we see and deduce for ourselves, or
what God tells us. The thrust of Abdiel's entire rebuttal to Satan is really
no rebuttal at all but rather the attempt to re-establish the priorities that
Satan's empiricism has overthrown. God, Abdiel can only repeat, is not
beholden to any exterior law; He is the *sine qua non*.

   Satan reveals his empirical commitment even more blatantly when
he challenges Abdiel's assertion that "by his Word the mighty Father made
/ All things, ev'n thee . . . ." (V, 836–837). Unwilling to accept even this
fundamental dogma, Satan remains unconvinced without "the ocular
proof":

> That we were form'd then say'st thou? and the work
> Of secondary hands, by task transferr'd
> From Father to his Son? strange point and new
>   . . .who saw
> When this creation was? remember'st thou
> Thy making, while the Maker gave thee being? (V, 853–858)

Having asked the empirical question, Satan supplies his own empirical
answer:

> We know no time when we were not as now;
> Know none before us, self-begot, self-raised
> By our own quick'ning power . . . (V, 859–861)

   The pattern of Satan's regression from "right" to "natural" reason is
rather ironically capsulized by Satan himself in Book Six where he
recollects for us his "progress" from religious misconception to empirical
"enlightenment":

> At first I thought that liberty and Heav'n
> To heav'nly Souls had been all one; but now
> I see that most through sloth had rather serve,
> Minist'ring Spirits, train'd up in Feast and Song. (VI, 164–167)

Satan's fall to "enlightenment" is paralleled by a concomitant fall of his language. Whereas "right" reason knows no double meanings to words, the advent of "natural" reasoning immediately ushers in legions of strange new connotations for old words. Where "service" originally meant the natural function of love, Satan now defines it as the inevitable consequence of sloth. Throughout *Paradise Lost* we discover Milton employing similar dualisms, persuading us that along with Satan's fall, diction falls too: "love" descends to "sloth," "obedience" stoops to "servility," "freedom" drops to "slavery." Satan's apostasy, in fact, introduces the possibility of God-talk into the universe, although on Satan's lips its logological doubleness characteristically flattens into literalism.

The consistency of Satan's empirical language orientation is clear throughout the epic, and his characterization of the ensuing battle in heaven as a contention between the "servility" of the faithful angels and the "freedom" of his own hordes is in perfect keeping here. Milton's determination to include Abdiel in the scene, however, is really what saves the hermeneutical potential of the situation, its religiously evocative power. Not Satan's argument, not Abdiel's argument, but the contention between them is the true hermeneutical yield of the debate. The debate is functionally parallel to Max Black's "interaction" metaphor: it brings the "two separate domains" of Satan's and Abdiel's language games "into cognitive and emotional relation by using language directly appropriate to the one as a lens for seeing the other."[2] It does this by permitting key words to be shared. But the sharing is of a very special sort, for rather than initiating a detente between the two hostile domains, it maintains their logical immiscibility by forcing new denotations upon key words. Just as God's "Golden Scepter" transmutes in Beelzebub's fallen mind to an "Iron Rod" (II, 327–328), so the meanings of theologically sensitive words change when their context is shifted from a "logic of obedience" to a "logic of empiricism."

The most volatile of the shared words is "freedom," and Milton cleverly balances the Christian sense of the word (". . . that whereby WE ARE LOOSED AS IT WERE BY ENFRANCHISEMENT, THROUGH CHRIST OUR DELIVERER, FROM THE BONDAGE OF SIN, AND CONSEQUENTLY FROM THE RULE OF THE LAW AND OF MAN; TO THE INTENT THAT BEING MADE SONS INSTEAD OF SERVANTS, AND PERFECT MEN INSTEAD OF CHILDREN, WE MAY SERVE GOD IN LOVE"[3]) against its quite distinct counterpart, "freedom" in the sense of one's liberty *from constraints*. One freedom is characterized by the positive thrust of "to" (freedom *to* "serve God in love"), while the other implies mere negative immunity from constraint (freedom *from* divine obligation).

Predictably, the "freedom speeches" of Abdiel and Satan conflict like two poles of a paradox, and the significant feature of the debate, from the point of view of God-talk, is that the resultant paradox is not resolved but left to stand. The paradox encloses and protects the crucial mystery of the Christian faith against literalism. Satan's understanding of freedom serves as a lens through which we gain intuitive insight into Abdiel's freedom. Because the debate makes secular non-sense, we are invited to adjust our orientation so that it will yield sacred wisdom. We can do this, of course, only by supplanting our empirical objectivity with the logic of obedience.

The Abdiel-Satan debate, then, not only says but *does* something to our orientation toward the event, and for that reason it qualifies as the sort of performative situation that characterizes genuine God-talk. Brilliant as it is in itself, the debate also provides the logical template for the War in Heaven, although, as we shall see, it is only one template of many, for Milton's exploitation of the logic of encounter is ubiquitous in the poem.

A more systematic and aggressive exploitation of the logic of encounter, in fact, takes place in the separation scene in Book Nine when Eve spiritedly challenges Adam for permission to divide their labors. This Miltonic addition to the Scriptural account of the Fall has intrigued critics not only because it is a charmingly rendered instance of domestic discord, but because it seems to bear the portentous imprint of a parable. There is a vividness, a strangeness, a realism about it that has "teased" many critical minds "into active thought" about its propriety. The vivid realism of Eve's femininity in particular seems to many readers to jar with the innocent decorum of Eden. Basil Willey defends the scene's propriety by arguing that it humanizes the sterile innocence of Paradise.[4] But humanizing the innocent couple also implies sanctioning a prevenient fallenness, an implication which has been seized and accepted by a number of critics.[5]

Some have suggested that the perfection of Adam and Eve is a growing rather than a completed state of being, thereby exonerating the "humanizing" symptoms of inchoate vanity and curiosity from the onus of an anticipatory fallenness.[6] The success of Milton's alleged humanizing effort with Eve is apparently so great that many critics have gallantly run to her defense by questioning Adam's behavior as a husband and mentor. Tillyard, for example, wanted Adam to take a more disciplinary stance toward Eve's coquettish ways by forcing her to stay by his side if all other argument failed.[7] Fredson Bowers, whom we shall have more to say about later, concurs that Adam should forcefully put his foot down and refuse Eve's request; Anthony Low also agrees.[8]

John Peter heaps scorn on Adam for his shortcomings as a debator. He wonders why Milton seems to make Adam so inept at parrying Eve's arguments. After noting that "every point [Eve] advances is lucid and persuasive — a fact which greatly enhances the demureness of her replies," he then contends that "Adam's rejoinders are deliberately made to seem inferior so that this advantage will remain with her."[9] He sympathizes with Adam's embarrassed reluctance to admit that he feels "doubtful about her ability to stand alone," but he is forced to trace how this reluctance leads first to the suggestion that they should "avoid / Th'attempt itself, intended by our Foe" (IX, 294–295) and then to the embarrassingly silly argument that even a temptation that fails "asperses / The tempted with dishonor foul" (IX, 296–297). Eve's rebuttal to this is devastating: ". . . his foul esteem / Sticks no dishonour on our Front, but turns / Foul on himself" (IX, 329–331). Peter also points out Adam's blunder when he asks, "Why shouldst not thou . . . thy trial choose / With me, best witness of the Virtue tr'd" (IX, 315–317), not seeing, as she does, that the trial is then no trial at all." It is not necessary to belabor the point other than to grant Mr. Peter that Adam's apparent ineptness here must have been deliberate on Milton's part. This is so manifestly true that we hardly balk at Peter's conclusion that Eve "holds the aces of reason" and Adam "the trumps of intuition."[10] But what a curious anomaly. Why should Milton concoct a debate that has the effect of reversing a psychological pattern that the rest of the epic has worked so hard to promote? Must we sadly document a Miltonic blunder, or should we examine the validity of this orientation towards the conversation?

Fredson Bowers is satisfied with Adam's argument, but he is disturbed by the abruptness with which he "caves in" to Eve, after having apparently won his case with the formidable challenge:

> Wouldst thou approve thy constancie, approve
> First thy obedience. (IX, 367–368)

"If he had stopped there," Bowers contends, "Eve could have had no answer, and we would still be innocent . . . After this firm assertion of his hierarchical duty to command and she to obey, he suddenly appears to cave in"[11]: "Go; for thy stay, not free, absents thee more" (IX, 372).

In addition to these objections to Adam's argumentative behavior, we might consider the propriety of Eve's language in the quarrel. Joan Bennett notes that "Eve is no mean reasoner and that her logic is highly sophisticated,"[12] but by almost any standard, her language in this episode is hardly consistent with her previous discourse in the epic. Here she speaks an apostate language indistinguishable from Satan's. Like Satan, for example, she bases her remarks upon a "sense of injur'd merit" (IX, 98). Miffed at what she interprets as a rebuke to her constancy, she begins a line of reasoning which, if we examine its logical underpinnings, is totally alien to the principles of theological objectivity we have learned to expect from her in her earlier speeches. Her remarks cleave to the authority of an autonomous virtue rather than God's will. She presses a humanistically laudable (but theologically spurious) trial of ethical virtue. Like Satan's, her language presumes a self-sufficiency inappropriate to her status. Her "objectivity towards the Truth," to use Torrance's term, has unaccountably shifted to an empirical base.

Equally Satanic is the fact that her language discloses the first symptoms of semantic duality which we have seen to be a linguistic concomitant to apostasy. Most noticeably Eve assigns a new meaning to the word "freedom." Where before she habitually understood it to describe a state of loving obedience, she now demands "freedom" *from* the moral constraints of her lover. She speaks the proud, humanistic ethic of *Areopagitica*, clearly disavowing the "fugitive and cloistered virtue" which divine edict, up to this point, had prescribed as best for her. Eve's language game, as we will see, is a linguistic novelty in Paradise.

These three apparent anomalies in the separation scene—that Adam, even though he is highest in intellectual endowment, argues less effectively than Eve; that Adam does not seem to behave as the Lord of Creation by "caving in" to Eve; that Eve speaks like a fallen woman before her technical lapse—nourish the nagging suspicion that more is going on here than meets the dramatically oriented eye. Joan Bennett, for example, has pierced beyond mere narrative concerns to suggest that the separation scene is Milton's "answer to the epistemological question that faced ethical antinomianism," arguing that "in Milton's view the first persons who had to deal with this dilemma of total spiritual liberty were unfallen man and woman, that the separation scene concerns not only relations between the sexes but the basic nature of human government."[13] Later our argument will take a somewhat similar tack, that an original dilemma is dealt with in the scene, but it will not contend that the subject of the domestic spat is the "nature of human government," but rather the nature of God's. But first, we should address the dramatic anomalies.

Taking the second anomaly first, we must agree with Bowers that Adam seems to violate the rule of hierarchy by "caving in" to Eve, but only so long as we view the situation from the narrow and incomplete point of view of hierarchy alone. In focusing our concern on the God-talk of *Paradise Lost* we have been only marginally concerned with patterns of ethics, hierarchies, and social mores, recognizing that more often than not such patterns serve merely as models awaiting theological qualification. The separation scene is not based solely on the principle of hierarchy, despite what Bowers and C.S. Lewis[14] contend. The theological dimension of the scene includes at least such additional considerations as the principle of Christian liberty to which Adam, at this point in the epic, is beholden. Does "authority" in a prelapsarian world function the same way it does in a fallen world? Bowers insists that it does, but is it not true that *Paradise Lost* teaches the opposite throughout? Everywhere in the epic we are shown that the significance of obedience is that it is *freely* bestowed, not demanded. God Himself states the principle:

> Not free, what proof could they have giv'n sincere
> Of true allegiance, constant Faith or Love,
> Where only what they needs must do, appear'd,
> Not what they would? (III, 103–106)

Following the logic of "Hee for God only, shee for God in him" (IV, 299), Eve's obedience to Adam must be equally dependent upon freedom as Adam's to God. For Adam to *force* Eve's will by making her stay, as Bowers recommends, would be to violate a fundamental principle of prelapsarian liberty. From the theological standpoint, "To; for thy stay, not free, absents thee more" (IX, 372) is not "bad doctrine" at all; it is a statement of a man whose hand has been forced by the very best of doctrines: Christian liberty.

The other two anomalies also respond to a proper theological perspective. Peter's impression of the argument, we recall, held Eve's to be the reasonable voice and Adam's the intuitional, an anomalous situation from any point of view. But suppose we seriously consider the logical similarity of Eve's and Satan's discourse and adopt a theological perspective toward the separation which recognizes its apostate configuration? Despite our "feelings" about the scene, which Peter no doubt accurately describes, we know that Eve is wrong in her intention to leave Adam and that Adam is right to want her to stay. Yet the structure and tone of the argument suggest the opposite: the "reasonable" course of action is apostasy; the "unreasonable," obedience. It is as if Milton were deliberately setting form and content, reason and faith, at cross-purposes.

The pattern should be familiar, for it recalls the "unbearable collision of values" that Waldock insists Adam experienced when he had to choose between Eve and God, just as it should also recall the "collision of values" in the Abdiel-Satan debate. The resolution of the apparent problem should also be familiar, for it demands our acknowledgement that in the separation scene, as in all scenes of apostasy in *Paradise Lost*, two conflicting language games are deliberately brought into close encounter for the purpose of adding a theological third dimension to the two-dimensional ethical model.

Let us examine more closely how these conflicting language games create a religiously illuminating logic of encounter in Adam and Eve's quarrel. Assuming Eve's language to be apostate in structure, we might expect that, like Satan's most persuasive speeches, it will follow "natural" instead of "right" reason, and that it will commit to an empirical objectivity. Similarly, we would expect Adam's language to reflect an objectivity toward the truth which holds as it authority obedience to God. To appreciate the logical conflict that these two linguistic commitments involve, we should bear in mind Torrance's axioms that "rationality in theological matters does not oppose . . . but presupposes obedience" and that "the appropriate act" in theological matters "is to *avoid* using 'ordinary' objectivity."[15] Seen in this light, the separation scene may perhaps yield fewer ethical improprieties than supposed and may reveal the reason why Milton was determined to have Eve "appear" the more engaging in the quarrel. In short, Peter's feeling that Eve speaks reason and Adam intuition and that although "both are right . . . Adam is righter because events will prove him so," may not be "paradoxical" in quite the way he thinks. It may be the case that Adam's speeches only *seem* to be based on intuition because their logical authority is not empirical. If this is true, what we are considering is a semantic rebellion on Eve's part which prepares and foreshadows a more credible temptation and fall than otherwise might have been possible if her language had not been permitted to lapse in advance. As it is, she meets Satan on an argumentative level that is common to both. Like the Believer in the parable of the Invisible Gardener, Eve finds herself arguing according to the rules of Satan's language game and her obedience (that "fine brash hypothesis"[16]) is "killed by inches, the death of a thousand qualifications." Both Eve's and Satan's objectivity toward the Truth is thoroughly empirical.[17]

The pattern is set from the very beginning of the argument when Eve looks about the garden and says to Adam

> the work under our labor grows,
> Luxurious by restraint; what we by day
> Lop overgrown, or prune, or prop, or bind,
> One night or two with wanton growth derides
> Tending to wild. (IX, 208–212)

There should be no question about the accuracy of her observation since Milton, only a few lines before, has clearly told us that the "work outgrew / The hands' dispatch of two Gard'ning so wide." Eve's empirical observation leads immediately to her pragmatic recommendation:

> Let us divide our labors, thou where choice
> Leads thee, or where most needs . . .
>   while I
> In yonder Spring of Roses intermix
> With Myrtle, find what to redress till Noon. (IX, 214–219)

and the recommendation is supported by empirical evidence of a
psychological nature:

> For while so near each other thus all day
> Our task we choose, what wonder if so near
> Looks intervene and smiles, or object new
> Casual discourse draw on, which intermits
> Our day's work brought to little, though begun
> Early, and th'hour of Supper comes unearn'd. (IX, 220–225)

Not only does Eve display a new "knowingness" in this speech, which
suggests some progress on the way from innocence to experience, but the
practical ordering of her priorities introduces a note into Paradise which
we today identify as the "Protestant work ethic." No sin has been officially
committed; Eve's innocence has in no way been overtly compromised, but
her language, because of its empirical orientation, establishes the
inevitability of things to come.

Understandably, Adam is confused by the surprisingly new tone of
Eve's discourse, and this probably accounts for the clumsiness with which
he deals with it. He begins by praising her practicality, however
patronizingly (it is good that woman "study household good" [IX, 233]
and try to promote "good works in her Husband" [IX, 234]), but the
theological objectivity of his stance requires him almost immediately to
set about restoring a similar theological objectivity in Eve's thinking:

> Yet not so strictly hath our Lord impos'd
> Labor, as to debar us when we need
> Refreshment . . .
> For not to irksome toil, but to delight
> He made us, and delight to Reason join'd. (IX, 235–243)

God's will, not the unruly luxuriance of Eden, should dictate human
conduct, Adam feels. His theological objectivity confronts and supplants
Eve's empirical objectivity. At this point the issue in Adam's mind is not
separation itself, but the motive for it. He sees a perilous significance in
the fact that Eve is employing as her authority for objectivity an apparent
empirical necessity: the garden needs more pruning. This is why he is
willing to allow Eve to go off by herself provided her motive is not
horticultural necessity:

> But if much converse perhaps
> Thee satiate, to short absence I could yield.
>   (IX, 248–249)

Under these conditions Eve's departure would not violate Adam's logic of
obedience and he can freely give his consent.

The danger of Satan's imminence, however, is another consideration and, as we search Adam's speeches for theological objectivity toward this threat, we are rewarded with lines which unfortunately cause us to wince at their patronizing, unheroic tone:

> The wife, where danger of dishonor lurks,
> Safest and seemliest by her husband stays,
> Who guards her, or with her the worst endures.
> (IX, 267–269)

The rules of this language game are much more arbitrary and much less appealing than those which we will see to govern Eve's. Nevertheless, they are the only *appropriate* rules for Edenic discourse. This is the text against which theological objectivity measures all things. The text for empirical objectivity, as Eve's and Satan's speeches abundantly show, can be found on any page of *Areopagitica*.

What about the "unkindness" that Eve allegedly meets in Adam's initial reply to her suggestion? Does it really exist, or is Eve, like Beelzebub and Satan, looking at a golden scepter and perceiving an iron rod? There is no question that Eve's speeches, like Satan's, reflect a sense of "injur'd merit." The "firmness" of her "Faith and Love," she feels, has been put into question by Adam's alleged implication that it can be "shak'n or seduc't" (IX, 257). But if we carefully examine Adam's speeches up to this point, we discover no such implication at all. To the contrary, he merely expresses the strong probability that Satan

> Watches, no doubt, with greedy hope to find
> His wish and best advantage, us asunder,
> Hopeless to circumvent us join'd, where each
> To other speedy aid might lend at need. (IX, 257–260)

Adam's emphasis is upon the *mutual* strength they share together and the *mutual* vulnerability they would risk apart. The only conceivable source for Eve's "injur'd merit" would seem to be Adam's articulation of the doctrine that the "Wife . . . Safest and seemliest by her Husband stays," and this Adam is duty-bound to recite in accordance with the logic of obedience. Eve clearly plays a new language game, and if the rules of that game produce sentiments and principles to which we respond because, to use Peter's words, of their "quiet good sense," it is only because we share the very same rules; our authority for objectivity is empirical fact too. When Eve stands up to her husband and retorts:

> And what is Faith, Love, Virtue, unassay'd
> Alone, without exterior help sustain'd? (IX, 335–336)

our humanistic sensibilities respond. We think of the rolling phrases from *Areopagitica:*

> I cannot praise a fugitive and cloistered virtue,
> unexercised and unbreathed, that never sallies out and sees
> her adversary, but slinks out of the race where that
> immortal garland is to be run for . . .

but fail, perhaps, to consider the authority for our objectivity as we applaud.

Patiently, almost doggedly, Adam replies to Eve's harangues with: "O Woman, best are all things as the will / Of God ordain'd them" (IX, 343–344) and "Seek not temptation . . . Trial will come unsought. / Wouldst thou approve thy constancie, approve / First thy obedience" (IX, 364–368). This is the litany of obedience. Its objectivity is divine; its reason is "right."

Adam's awkwardness in the separation scene is largely the result of Milton's strategy to exploit the logic of encounter. His apparent argumentative ineptitude is mostly just that—apparent. The claims of right reason and the claims of natural reason are given their day on the field to battle it out with one another. Nevertheless, it is difficult to suppress the suspicion that even though Milton's Adam is rhetorically hampered by the logic of obedience, depriving his speeches of the winsomeness of a more humanistically oriented discourse, he could have done better than he did. Peter's feeling that "Adam's rejoinders are deliberately made to seem inferior" is well taken. Why did Milton give the advantage to Eve?

The answer to this nagging question is perhaps lodged in a pattern we have discovered as consistent in all the apostasy situations in *Paradise Lost*—a pattern in which deeply felt ethical convictions of human beings are deliberately juxtaposed against theological principles which contradict them. Adam's dilemma between chivalry and divine obligation, Satan's heroic manifestos in favor of civil liberty, Eve's confident uncloistered virtue versus Adam's cautious obedience, all these conflicts seem designed to shock readers out of their secular, ethical complacencies into a realization that religious obedience, as Milton defines it in the *Christian Doctrine*, "is that virtue whereby we propose to ourselves the will of God as the *paramount* rule of our conduct, and serve him alone" [Italics added].

But there is another reason why Milton may have found it to his advantage to make Eve's side of the quarrel seem the more attractive of the two. A linguistically and ethically obedient Eve would, like the Lady in *Comus*, be "clad in compleat steel." Eve's linguistic chastity would more than justify the Lady's confident challenge to Comus: "Fool do not boast. Thou canst not touch the freedom of my minde" (ll. 662–663). Milton was at pains to create circumstances whereby Satan *could* touch the freedom of Eve's mind, but as long as she was firmly committed to a logic of obedience this would be impossible. A linguistically chaste Eve might conceivably be bewildered by Satan's blandishments (having never heard such strange logic in Paradise before) just as Adam was apparently bewildered by hers, but, committed to disparate language games, she and Satan could hardly be expected to affect one another persuasively. No common objectivity toward the Truth brings their dialogue into consonance.

To put the issue bluntly, it seems plausible to assume that Milton calculated a *linguistic* fall for Eve prior to her actual lapse. It appears to be a necessary contrivance in order to preserve the credibility of her temptation under the tree, but it is a contrivance that is brilliantly and subtly camouflaged by Eve's overwhelmingly attractive humanism. As we hear her enthusiastically suing for her rights as a free individual with all the rhetorical competence that the consummately experienced Milton can give her, we can hardly be expected to maintain in our minds simultaneously that she is nevertheless dead wrong. The very basis of her appeal for us—her self-confidence—is precisely what makes her vulnerable to Satan's tempting. Even before they meet under the tree, Eve and Satan have reached an understanding. God's arbitrary decree is no longer for either tempter nor tempted the authority for objectivity toward the Truth; the new authority hangs on a branch above their heads.

Proof that Eve's language has switched its logical character from theological to empirical objectivity can be had simply by comparing her speeches before and after the quarrel with Adam. How different Eve seems even as late as Book Eight when she retires from the conversation with Adam and Raphael because "her huband the Relater she preferr'd / Before the Angel, and of him to ask / Chose rather" (VIII, 52–54). But perhaps even more telling than this example of obedient, willing capitulation to hierarchy is the contrast between Eve's attitudes toward Eden's plenty in Book Five, where

> earth's hallow'd mould,
> Of God inspir'd . . .
> shall confess that here on Earth
> God hath dispenst his bounties as in Heav'n (V, 321–330)

and Book Nine, where, as we have seen, the divine *gift* of plenitude has subtly changed to an *obligation*:

> Luxurious by restraint; what we by day
> Lop overgrown, or prune, or prop, or bind,

> One night or two with wanton growth derides
> Tending to wild. (IX, 208–212)

Prior to the quarrel, Eve's language consistently corresponded with an appropriate theological objectivity unusually manifesting itself in a relentless subordination of empirical evidence to the higher authority of God's decrees (generally transmitted to her through Adam). Indeed, Eve's first speech in the epic makes this abundantly clear:

> O thou for whom
> And from whom I was form'd flesh of thy flesh,
> And without whom am to no end, my Guide
> And Head, what thou hast said is just and right. (IV, 440–443)

Eve appears almost to revel in submission when she goes on to admit that she enjoys

> So far the happier Lot, enjoying thee
> Preeminent by so much odds, while thou
> Like consort to thyself canst nowhere find. (IV, 445–448)

This is clearly not the same girl who chafes in Book Nine at her "Guide / and Head'[s]" conviction that "The Wife . . . Safest and seemliest by her Husband stays." Something has happened to Eve's orientation toward the Truth and, consequently, her status.

It is a literal and thoroughly empirical Eve, then, who talks with Satan under the tree — an Eve highly impressionable to the evidence of the senses. Her first words, in fact, express amazement at an empirical anomaly:

> What may this mean? Language of Man pronounc't
> By Tongue of Brute, and human sense exprest? (IX, 553–554)

In the succeeding two lines Milton leads Eve to create an unmistakable conflict between theological and empirical authorities:

> The first at least of these I thought deni'd
> To Beasts, whom God on thir Creation-Day
> Created mute to all articulate sound. (IX, 555–557)

Eve has been confronted with a test: Will she choose appearances as a guide to her understanding, or divine decrees and instruction? With Baconian enthusiasm she seeks an empirical explanation:

> Redouble then this miracle, and say,
> How cam'st thou speakable of mute . . . (IX, 562–563)

This, of course, provides the opportunity for Satan to expound upon the magical properties of the Tree of Knowledge, a view toward the tree against which Basil Willey properly cautioned.[18]

Eve still maintains a certain healthy skepticism, but following an empirical lead, asks to be *shown* the evidence: "But say, where grows the Tree, from hence how far?" (IX, 617) As soon as she recognizes which tree it is, her empirical orientation is momentarily challenged by the theological:

> Serpent, we might have spar'd our coming hither
> Fruitless to mee, though Fruit be here to excess . . .
> But of this Tree we may not taste nor touch:
> God so commanded, and left that Command
> Sole Daughter of his Voice . . . (IX, 647–653)

The issue is once again before us: which ought to have the higher claim upon us, obedience or appearances — faith or reason? But in spite of Eve's promising recognition and acknowledgement of the tree and its prohibition, and despite Milton's insistent interjection that Eve is "yet sinless" (IX, 659), it is quite evident that her demonstrated predilection for empirical rather than theological confirmation renders the persuasiveness of Satan's propositions and demonstrations irresistible.

Satan invokes the tree as the "Mother of Science" and acknowledges its power "not only to discern / Things in thir Causes but to trace the ways of highest Agents" (IX, 680–683). In Satan's mind the reversal of the priorities between natural reason and right reason is complete. The "Mother of Science" empowers him to comprehend existence as a vast, traceable network of cause-and-effect relationships. In subordinating the "ways of highest Agents" to scientific explanation, Satan echoes the attempts of the empiricists, whom Raphael satirizes in Book Eight, "To save appearances" (VIII, 83).

Against Eve's objections that the Tree has been interdicted and that the consequence of death awaits disobedience, Satan bluntly replies, ". . . do not believe / Those rigid threats of Death; ye shall not Die" (IX, 684–685). For confirmation, he points to himself:

> look on mee,
> Mee who have touch'd and tasted, yet both live,
> And life more perfet have attain'd than Fate
> Meant mee, by vent'ring higher than my Lot. (IX, 687–690)

Eve is the opposite of the Paduan professor Basil Willey describes, who "refused to look through Galileo's telescope" because he wished to avoid a collision between metaphysical truth and empirical fact.[19] She is

predisposed to pick up the "telescope" Satan offfers and assess the
situation with impeccable scientific disinterestedness:

> Great are thy Virtues, doubtless, best of Fruits,
> Though kept from Man, and worthy to be admired,
> Whose taste, too lang forborne, at first assay
> Gave elocution to the mute, and taught
> The Tongue not made for Speech to speak they praise.
>   (IX, 745–749)

Theological "conclusions" are arrived at through empirical methods: the
fruit is "worthy to be admired" and has been "kept from Man." While the
apple is certainly a fine one, and while God has indeed "kept" Mankind
from eating it, the context within which these assertions are made — a
scientific one — makes the implications tyrannical and sinister. Even the
theologically respectable concept of covenant is perversely tainted by the
empirical context in which it is placed. Eve argues:

> In plain, then, what forbid he but to know,
> Forbids us good, forbids us to be wise?
> Such prohibitions bind not. (IX, 758–760)

An empirical rather than a theological "good" dictates the breach of
contract here, and the echo in these lines of *The Tenure of Kings and
Magistrates* should once again call to our minds the absurdity of applying
ethics appropriate to men to God. But this is precisely what Satan does,
and Eve literally falls for it. Why? Because she has been made a literalist.
Her empirically-oriented mind has been tricked by "appearances": that the
serpent who speaks to her under the tree really *is* a serpent.

Eve's blindness, regrettably, is too often our blindness when we
read religious works such as *Paradise Lost*. An ambivalent attitude
toward the *function* of most Christian texts keeps us from experiencing
evocations of truly religious mystery which anthropomorphic models
normally are intended to initiate. We settle for the penultimate
achievement of the artist — the model itself — rather than opening our
sensibilities to that toward which the model points. The price we pay for
this semantic idolatry is that sooner or later the loose threads, the
inconsistencies, the breaches of decorum and the annoying conundrums,
that works such as *Paradise Lost* yield when they are not read as God-
talk, accumulate to the point where we can no longer responsibly blame
Milton for them. At that time we may entertain the possibility that we do
not know how to read God-talk as rewardingly as we might, and we
might even be goaded into trying to learn.

Notes

Chapter 1: Introduction

1. W.H. Auden, "Postscript: Christianity and Art," *The Dyer's Hand and Other Essays* (New York: Random House, 1962), p. 456.

2. John Maquarrie, *God-Talk: An Examination of the Language and Logic of Theology* (London: SCM, 1967), p. 11.

3. David Crystal and Derek Davy, *Investigating English Style*, English Language Series (London: Longmans, 1969), p. 166.

4. Mircea Eliade, *The Sacred and the Profane: The Nature of Religion*, trans. Willard R. Trask (New York and London: Harcourt Brace Jovanovich, 1959), p. 13.

5. T.S. Eliot, "Religion and Literature," *Selected Essays* (New York: Harcourt Brace Jovanovich, Inc., 1950), p. 346.

6. A.J.A. Ayer, *Language, Truth and Logic*, 2nd. ed. (New York: Dover, 1946), p. 120.

7. H.R. Swardson, *Poetry and the Fountain of Light* (London: George Allen & Unwin, 1962), p. 147.

8. Jean Ladrière, *Language and Belief*, trans. Garrett Barden (Notre Dame: University of Notre Dame Press, 1972), p. 7.

9. Carl Michalson, *Worldly Theology: The Hermeneutical Focus of an Historical Faith* (New York: Scribners, 1967), p. 46.

10. John Wisdom, "Gods," *Logic and Language (First Series)*, ed. Antony Flew (Oxford: Basil Blackwell, 1955), pp. 192–193).

11. A.G.N. Flew and A. MacIntyre, eds., *New Essays in Philosophical Theology* (London: SCM, 1955), p. 96

12. The phrase comes from C.H. Dodd's classic definition of the parable, which is discussed in later chapters. He stresses the open-endedness of the parable form by concluding that it leaves the mind "in sufficient doubt about its precise application to tease it into active thought" (C.H. Dodd, *The Parables of the Kingdom*, rev. ed. [New York: Scribners, 1961], p. 16).

13. Flew, *New Essays*, p. 96.

14. Wisdom, *Logic and Language*, p. 191.

15. Walter Raleigh, *Milton* (New York: Benjamin Blom, 1967), p. 85.

16. A.J.A. Waldock, *Paradise Lost and Its Critics* (Cambridge, Cambridge University Press, 1966), pp. 55–56.

17. *William Perkins: 1558–1602,* ed. Thomas F. Merrill (Nieuwkoop: De Graaf, 1966), p. 11.

18. *Logic and Language* p. 200.

19. Erich Auerbach, *Mimesis: The Representation of Reality in Western Literature,* trans. Willard Trask (Princeton: Princeton University Press, 1953), pp. 4–19.

20. Quoted by Richard Hooker in *Of the Laws of Ecclesiastical Polity,* 2 vols. (London: J.M. Dent & Sons, 1960), II, p. 69.

21. William Perkins, *The Arte of Prophecying. Or A Treatise Concerning the Sacred and Onely True Manner and Methode of Preaching* (Cambridge: John Legate, 1609), p. 736.

22. Ibid., p. 754.

23. *The Sermons of John Donne,* ed. George R. Potter and Evelyn M. Simpson, 10 vols. (Berkeley: University of California Press, 1953–1962), VI, sermon 16, lines 653–654.

24. Perkins, *Prophecying,* p. 732.

25. John Milton, *The Reason of Church Government,* in *Complete Poems and Major Prose,* ed. Merritt Y. Hughes (New York: Odyssey, 1957), p. 671.

26. Ibid., p. 681.

27. Ibid., p. 669.

Chapter 2: Words About God

1. "First we have to look at grammar, for it is in fact of theological significance" *(Table Talk,* Weimar Edition 5; 27, 8).

2. Kenneth Burke, *The Rhetoric of Religion: Studies in Logology* (Berkeley, Los Angeles, London: University of California Press, 1970), p. vi.

3. Ian T. Ramsey, ed., *Words about God: The Philosophy of Religion* (New York, Evanston, San Francisco, London: Harper & Row, 1971). This collection of essays nicely charts the issue of religious language by first presenting the classical discussions (Plotinus through Rudolf Otto), then moving on to the empirical critique (Russell, Moore, early Wittgenstein and Ayer), continuing with more recent empiricist views (Ryle, Austin, Hare, Ogden and I.A. Richards) and concluding with exploratory essays on the logical character of religious language (Hepburn, Ramsey, Evans and Evans-Pritchard).

4. Burke, *Rhetoric of Religion,* p. 7.

5. Friedrich Waismann, "Language Strata," *Logic and Language (Second Series),* ed. A.G.N. Flew (Oxford: Basil Blackwell, 1966), p. 19.

6. Ibid., p. 21.

7. E.L. Mascall, *Words and Images: a Study in Theological Discourse* (London: Libra, 1968), p. 101.

8. Bertrand Russell, *Language and Reality* (London: George Allen and Unwin, 1939), p. 306.

9. See Flew, *New Essays,* p. 96.

10. I.M. Crombie, "The Possibility of Theological Statements," *Faith and Logic,* ed. Basil Mitchell, Oxford Essays in Philosophical Theology (London: George Allen & Unwin, 1957), p. 40.

11. John Macquarrie, for example, speaks of how the problem of how ordinary language might be "stretched so that one can use it to talk about God" *(God-talk,* p. 33), implicitly referring to such attempts as Ramsey's to "stretch" empirical models so as to render them appropriate currency for divine subject

matter (Ian T. Ramsey, *Religious Language: an Empirical Placing of Theological Phrases* [New York: Macmillan, 1957], pp. 55–102).

12. Crystal and Davy, *Investigating English Style*, pp. 165–166.

13. Gordon D. Kaufman, *God the Problem* (Cambridge, Mass.: Harvard University Press, 1972), p. 86.

14. Ibid., p. 85.

15. John Milton, *The Christian Doctrine*, "Of God," in *Complete Poems and Major Prose*, p. 905.

16. See S.I. Hayakawa, *Language in Thought and Action*, 3rd ed. (New York: Harcourt Brace Jovanovich, 1972), p. 27.

17. Ian T.Ramsey, "Logical Empiricism and Patristics," *studia Patristica V*, ed. F.L. Cross, Akadamie-Verlag (Berlin, 1962), p. 541. Also repr. in Ramsey, *Words about God*, p. 219.

18. Frederick Ferré, *Language, Logic and God* (New York: Harper & Row, 1969), p. 151.

19. Auerbach, *Mimesis:*, p. 4.

20. Ibid., p. 19.

21. Ibid., p. 9.

22. D.Z. Phillips, *The Concept of Prayer* (London: Routledge & Kegan Paul, 1965), p. 43.

23. Ramsey, *Religious Language* (see n. 11), p. 43.

24. Rudolph Bultmann, *Jesus Christ and Mythology* (New York: Scribners, 1958), p. 53.

25. Ramsey, *Religious Language*, p. 51.

26. Ramsey, *Religious Language*, p. 46.

Chapter 3: The Varieties of God-Talk

1. Ludwig Wittgenstein, *Tractatus Logico-Philosophicus*, trans. D.F. Pears and B.F. McGuinness (London: Routledge & Kegan Paul, 1961), 4.121.

2. I have in mind, of course, the work of such critics as J.M. Evans *(Paradise Lost and the Genesis Tradition)*, William Madsen *(From Shadowy Types to Truth)*, Joseph Wittreich *(Visionary Poetics)*, William Kerrigan *(The Prophetic Milton)*, Michael Lieb *(Poetics of the Holy)* and the like.

3. Dennis Burden, *The Logical Epic: a Study of the Argument of Paradise Lost* (Cambridge, Mass.: Harvard University Press, 1967), p. 1.

4. Gerhard Ebeling, *Introduction to a Theological Theory of Language*, trans. R.A. Wilson (London: William Collins Sons, 1973), p. 189.

5. Ibid., p. 86.

6. The term is Donald Evans'. His point is that "the basic 'ordinary' language to which an analytic philosopher should appeal when he considers *Christian* conceptions is biblical language" (Evans, *The Logic of Self-Involvement: A Philosophical Study of Everyday Language with Special Reference to the Christian Use of Language about God as Creator* [London: SCM, 1963], p. 17.

7. Ibid., p. 18.

8. Ferré, *Language, Logic and God*, p. 153.

9. Ibid.

10. Ebeling, *Theological Theory of Language*, p. 182.

11. Ramsey, *Religious Language*, p. 15.

12. Ian T. Ramsey, "Contemporary Empiricism," *The Christian Scholar* (Fall, 1960), 181.

13. Eliade, *The Sacred and the Profane*, p. 16.

14. Ramsey, *Religious Language*, pp. 15, 42.

15. Rudolf Otto, *The Idea of the Holy*, trans. John W. Harvey (Harmondsworth, Middlesex: Penguin, 1959), p. 19.

16. Ramsey registers his indebtedness to Joseph Butler's *The Analogy of Religion Natural and Revealed to the Constitution and Course of Nature* for the notion of "discernment-commitment" situations. "Butler suggests," says Ramsey, "that religion claims (a) a fuller discernment, to which we respond with (b) a total commitment. Such a commitment without any discernment whatever is bigotry and idolatry; to have the discernment without an appropriate commitment is the worst of all religious vices. It is insincerity and hypocrisy" *(Religious Language,* p. 19).

17. "If religious language has to talk about situations . . . which are perceptual with difference, perceptual and more," says Ramsey, "its language will be object language and more, i.e., object language which has been given very special qualifications, object language which exhibits logical peculiarities, logical impropriety" *(Religious Language,* p. 42).

18. Ramsey devotes the entirety of Chapter 2 of *Religious Language* to this process (pp. 55–102). The process Ramsey describes is remarkably similar to Rudolf Otto's account of "The Law of the Association of Feelings" in *The Idea of the Holy:* "I can pass from one feeling to another by an imperceptibly gradual transition, the one feeling x dying away little by little, while the other, y, excited together with it, increases and strengthens in a corresponding degree . . . . What passes over — undergoes transition — is not the feeling itself. It is not that the actual feeling gradually changes in quality or 'evolves', i.e. transmutes itself into a quite different one, but rather that *I* pass over or make the transition from one feeling to another as my circumstances change, by the gradual decrease of the one and increase of the other" (pp. 57–8).

19. See Ferré, *Language, Logic and God*, pp. 78–93.

20. John Hick, *Philosophy and Religion*, Foundations of Philosophy Series, ed. Elizabeth and Monroe Beardsley (Englewood Cliffs, N.J.: Prentice-Hall, 1963), P. 76.

21. Bertrand Russell, *Language and Reality*, p. 106.

22. References are to *John Milton: Complete Poems and Major Prose*, ed. Merritt Y. Hughes (New York: Odyssey Press, 1957).

23. *The Sermons of John Donne*, III, sermon 17, lines 407–13.

24. T.F. Torrance, "Faith and Philosophy," *The Hibbert Journal*, XLVII (1949), 237.

25. A *blik*, as R.M. Hare defines it, is not an assertion but a way of looking at something. He illustrates the notion by recounting the plight of a lunatic who is convinced that all Oxford dons want to murder him. The lunatic has a *blik* about dons. *Bliks* are not explanations, but, "as Hume saw, without a *blik* there can be no explanation; for it is by our *bliks* that we decide what is and what is not an explanation" (R.M. Hare, "Theology and Falsification," repr. in *New Essays in Philosophical Theology*, eds. Antony Flew and Alasdair McIntyre [New York: Macmillan, 1955], p. 101).

26. Torrance, "Faith and Philosophy," p. 273.

27. *The Works of George Herbert*, ed. F.E. Hutchinson (Oxford: Clarendon Press, 1967), p. 166.

28. Stanley Fish, *Self-Consuming Artifacts: The Experience of Seventeenth-Century Literature* (Berkeley: University of California Press, 1972), p. 173.

29. Ibid.

30. See Ferré, *Language, Logic and God*, p. 89.

31. Ibid.

32. I have in mind such performatively-based positions as John R. Searle's "Speech-Act theory" *(Speech Acts* [Cambridge: Cambridge University Press, 1969] and Ebeling's concern for the "act of utterance" *(Introduction to a Theological Theory of Language)*. Both positions challenge the view that "language is primarily descriptive in character" and maintain that "to describe the function of language as that of a sign is not sufficient," for the speech event does more; it "brings about an encounter with the subject itself" (Ebeling, p. 102).

33. Ebeling, *Theological Theory of Language*, p. 191.

34. Ibid.

35. Ibid., p. 192.

36. "A 'self-involving' utterance, in contrast with a 'flat' utterance," Evans explains, "is one in which the speaker does one or more of the following: he commits himself to future conduct or he implies that he has a particular attitude or he expresses a feeling or attitude. In a "flat" utterance, he does none of these" (Evans, *Faith and the Contemporary Epistemologies*, McMartin Memorial Lectures [Ottawa: Editions de l'Universite d'Ottawa, 1977], p. 12).

37. Evans, *Language of Self-Involvement*, p. 153.

38. Ibid., p. 128.

39. Milton, *The Christian Doctrine*, "Of God," in *Complete Poems and Major Prose*, p. 905.

40. Evans, *Logic of Self-Involvement*, p. 250.

41. Beda Allemann makes the interesting observation that "by avoiding metaphors that may be isolated as single stylistic figures here and there in the text, the parable as a whole is a kind of absolute metaphor." By "absolute," he means "a metaphor whose only frame of reference is itself" (Beda Allemann, "Metaphor and Antimetaphor," *Interpretation: The Poetry of Meaning*, eds. Stanley Romaine Hopper and David Miller [New York: Harcourt, Brace & World, 1967], p. 114).

42. C.H. Dodd, *Parables of the Kingdom*, p. 10.

43. Robert Ellrodt, "George Herbert and the Religious Lyric," *English Poetry and Prose 1540–1674*, ed. Christopher Ricks (London, 1970), p. 199.

44. *Cyclopedia of Biblical, Theological, and Ecclesiastical Literature*, ed. John McClintock and James Strang (New York: Harper and Bros., 1877), VII, p. 644.

45. Max Black, *Models and Metaphors* (Ithaca, N.Y.: Cornell University Press, 1962), p. 46.

46. The words are Robert Funk's, *Language, Hermeneutic, and the Word of God* (New York: Harper & Row, 1966), p. 140.

47. Ibid., p. 152.

48. Evans, *Logic of Self-Involvement*, p. 232. Corroboration of Evans' view can be found in Edwyn Bevan's *Symbolism and Belief* (London, 1938): "The Theist or Christian does not merely say: 'Act as if there were a God who is a loving Father, and you will find certain desirable results follow' (that is Pragmatism): he says, 'Act as if there were a God who is a loving Father, and you will, in doing, be making the right response to that which God really is. God is really of such a character that, if any of us could know Him as He is (which we cannot do) and then had to describe in human language to man upon earth what we saw, he

would have to say: 'What I see is undescribable, but if you think of God as a loving Father, I cannot put the reality to you in a better way than that: that is the nearest you can get" (pp. 335–6).

49. Crystal and Davy, *Investigating English Style*, p. 167.

50. Rudolf Otto charges Fichte and Schopenhauer with this form of idolatry: ". . . both these writers are guilty of the same error that is already found in myth; they transfer 'natural' attributes, which ought to be used as 'ideograms' for what is itself properly beyond utterance, to the non-rational as real qualifications of it, and they mistake symbolic expressions of feelings for adequate concepts upon which a 'scientific' structure of knowledge may be based" (Otto, *The Idea of the Holy*, p. 38).

51. Geddes MacGregor, *Aesthetic Experience in Religion* (London: Macmillan, 1947), p. 213. C.S. Lewis adds interesting support to MacGregor's position: "The Christian will take literature a little less seriously than the cultured Pagan. . . . The unbeliever is always apt to make a kind of religion of his aesthetic experiences." (C.S. Lewis, "Christianity and Literature," *Rehabilitations and Other Essays* [Oxford: Oxford University Press, 1939], p. 195).

52. Walter Kaufmann, *Critique of Religion and Philosophy* (New York: Anchor, 1961), p. 368.

Chapter 4: Hell and Heaven

1. Wittgenstein, *Tracatus Logico-Philosophicus*, 7.

2. See Isabel MacCaffrey, *Paradise Lost as "Myth,"* (Cambridge, Mass.: Harvard University Press, 1959), p. 44. Mrs. MacCaffrey's term "virtual myth" bears comparison with Beda Allemann's "absolute metaphor" ("Metaphor and Antimetaphor" [*see* chap. 3, p. 41], p. 114.

3. Kenneth Burke, *Rhetoric of Religion*, pp. 7–8.

4. Kenneth Burke, *Rhetoric of Religion*, p. 8.

5. Murray Roston, *Milton and the Baroque* (Pittsburgh: University of Pittsburgh Press, 1980), pp. 99, 100.

6. Edmund Burke, *A Philosophical Enquiry into the Origin of Our Ideas of the Sublime and the Beautiful*, ed. J.T. Boulton (Notre Dame and London: University of Notre Dame Press), p. 57.

7. Otto, *Idea of the Holy*, p. 78.

8. Otto, *Idea of the Holy*, p. 56.

9. Edmund Burke, *Philosophical Enquiry*, p. 59.

10. Ibid., p. 69.

11. Ibid., p. 71.

12. Ibid., p. 72.

13. Ibid., p. 73.

14. Otto, *Idea of the Holy*, p. 27.

15. Roland Frye, *Milton's Imagery and the Visual Arts: Iconographic Tradition in the Epic Poems* (Princeton: Princeton University Press, 1978), p. 149.

16. ". . . most English Protestants," says Frye, "probably objected in greater or lesser degree to visual delineation of God the Father, and most Puritans certainly did. As for the Godhead itself, Milton followed the precedents of his coreligionists and of the early Church in making the Son the only visual and operative principal of deity" (*Milton's Imagery*, p. 150).

17. Rudolf Bultmann, *Kerygma and Myth*, ed. H.W. Bartsch, trans. R.H. Fuller (New York: Harper Torchbook, 1961), p. 10, n. 2.

18. Martin Heidegger, *Unterwegs zur Sprache*, 2nd. ed. (Pfullingen, 1960), pp. 121f.

19. Schubert Ogden, *Christ Without Myth* (New York: Harper and Row, 1961), pp. 25–6.

20. John Donne, *The First Anniversarie*, "An Anatomie of the World," lines 279–83.

21. J.B. Broadbent, "Milton's Heaven," *Milton's Epic Poetry*, ed. C.A. Patrides (Harmondsworth, Middlesex: Penguin, 1967), p. 136.

22. Lord David Cecil, in *The Oxford Book of Christian Verse* (Oxford: Oxford University Press, 1940), p. xxi.

23. MacCaffrey, *Paradise Lost as "Myth"* (see n. 1), pp. 44–5.

24. Ibid., p. 39.

25. Allemann, "Metaphor and Antimetaphor," p. 114.

26. Anne Davidson Ferry, *Milton's Epic Voice: the Narrator in Paradise Lost* (Cambridge, Mass.: Harvard University Press, 1963), p. 6.

27. Ibid., p. 18.

28. MacCaffrey, *Paradise Lost as "Myth,"* p. 31. The idea of Milton as visionary seer conflicts rather specifically with his stated position in *The Christian Doctrine* that knowledge of God "far transcends the power of man's thoughts, much more of his perception . . ."

29. William Kerrigan, *The Prophetic Milton* (Charlottesville: University of Virginia Press, 1974).

30. See Joseph A. Wittreich, Jr., *Visionary Poetics: Milton's Tradition and his Legacy* (San Marino, Cal.: Huntington Library, 1957).

31. See Michael Lieb, *Poetics of the Holy: A Reading of Paradise Lost* (Chapel Hill: University of North Carolina Press, 1981), p. xix.

32. Lieb, *Poetics of the Holy*, p. xx.

33. William Madsen, *From Shadowy Types to Truth: Studies in Milton's Symbolism* (New Haven and London: Yale University Press, 1968), p. 82.

34. Ibid., p. 52.

35. Ibid.

36. Stanley Fish, *Surprised by Sin: The Reader in Paradise Lost* (London and New York: St. Martin's, 1967), p. 1.

37. See, for example, W. Fraser Mitchell, *English Pulpit Oratory from Andrewes to Tillotson* (London, 1932), or M.M. Knappen, *Tudor Puritanism* (Chicago, 1933). William Haller has much to say on the point throughout *The Rise of Puritanism* (New York: Harper Torchbook, 1957), esp. pp. 130–32.

38. *The Sermons of John Donne*, VI, sermon 1, lines 600–05.

39. Mascall, *Words and Images*, p. 109.

40. J.F. Bethune-Baker, *Introduction to the Early History of Christian Doctrine* (London Methuen, n.d.), p. 160. Quoted by Ian Ramsey, *Religious Language*, pp. 190–91.

41. C.A. Patrides, *Paradise Lost and the Language of Theology,"* *Language and Style in Milton*, eds. Ronald Emma and John T. Shawcross (New York: Ungar, 1967), pp. 102–19.

42. Ibid., p. 104.

43. Ibid., p. 105.

44. Ibid., p. 108.

45. Ibid., p. 110.

46. Peter Berek, " 'Plain' and 'Ornate' Styles and the Structure of *Paradise Lost,*" PMLA, LXXXV (March, 1970), 237.

47. Arnold Stein, *Answerable Style* (Minneapolis: University of Minnesota Press, 1953)m, p. 101.

48. Irene Samuels, "The Dialogue in Heaven: A Reconsideration of *Paradise Lost,* III, 1–417," PMLA LXII (September, 1957), 603.

49. Haller, *The Rise of Puritanism* (see n. 36), p. 132.

50. Fish, *Surprised by Sin,* pp. 61–2.

51. Broadbent, "Milton's Heaven," p. 144.

52. David Crystal, "The Language of Religion," in Crystal and Davy, *Investigating English Style,* p. 168.

53. Seymour Chatman, "Milton's Participial Style," *PMLA,* LXXXIII (October, 1968), 1398.

54. I use the terminology of Max Black *(Models and Metaphors):* "In making scale models our purpose is to reproduce, in a relatively manipulable or accessible embodiment, selected features of the 'original': we want to see how the new house will look, or to find out how the airplane will fly, or to learn how the chromosome changes occur. We try to bring the remote and the unknown to our own level of middle-sized existence . . . . An analogue model is some material object, system, or process designed to reproduce as faithfully as possible in some new medium the *structure* or web of relationship in an original" (pp. 221–222).

55. Joan Webber, *Milton and his Epic Tradition* (Seattle and London: University of Washington Press, 1979), p. 118.

56. Fish, *Surprised by Sin,* p. 74. The original observation is contained in James Sims, *The Bible in Milton's Epics* (Gainesville: University of Florida Press, 1962), p. 262.

57. See Auerbach, *Mimesis,* p. 8.

58. Quoted by Fish, *Surprised by Sin,* pp. 80–81.

59. Waismann, "Language Strata," p. 31.

60. MacCaffrey, *Paradise Lost as "Myth,"* p. 142.

61. Ferry, *Milton's Epic Voice,* p. 28.

62. MacCaffrey, *Paradise Lost as "Myth,"* p. 142.

63. Auerbach, *Mimesis,* p. 16.

Chapter 5: Milton's Satanic Parable

1. Burden, *The Logical Epic,* p. 1.

2. Waldock, *Paradise Lost and Its Critics,* p. 112.

Stein, *Answerable Style,* p. 128.

4. Louis Martz, *The Paradise Within* (New Haven, Conn.: Yale University Press, 1964), p. 119.

5. Fish, *Surprised by Sin,* p. 1.

6. See, for example, Berek, " 'Plain' and 'Ornate' Styles," p. 237ff.

7. Funk, *Language, Hermeneutic, and the Word of God,* p. 145.

8. In the defense of the propriety of Satan as an indirect communicator of religious awe, I cite Rudolf Otto's contention that one of the most effective indirect means of giving expression to the numinous is "the 'fearful' and horrible, and even at times the revolting and the loathsome. Inasmuch as the corresponding feelings are closely analogous to that of the *tremendum,* their outlets and means of expression may become indirect modes of expressing the specific 'numinous awe' that cannot be expressed directly" (Otto, *Idea of the Holy,* p. 77).

9. In describing biblical style, Auerbach concludes, ". . . the whole, permeated with the most unrelieved suspense and directed toward a single goal (and to that extent far more of a unity), remains mysterious and 'fraught with background' " (Auerbach, *Mimesis*, p. 9).

10. Chatman, "Milton's Participial Style," p. 1398.

11. See Berek, " 'Plain' and 'Ornate' Styles," p. 237ff.

12. F. Waismann, "Language Strata," p. 21.

13. Otto, *Idea of the Holy*, pp. 83–84.

Chapter 6: Performative Precepts

1. Wittgenstein, *Tractatus Logico-Philosophicus*, 6. 44.

2. Flew, *New Essays*, p. 173.

3. Milton, *The Christian Doctrine*, p. 973.

4. Kester Svendsen, *Milton and Science* (Cambridge: Harvard University Press, 1956), p. 43.

5. Walter Clyde Curry, *Milton's Ontology, Cosmogony, and Physics* (Lexington: University of Kentucky Press, 1957), p. 10.

6. Svendsen, *Milton and Science*, p. 5.

7. Auerbach, *Mimesis*, p. 4.

8. Ibid., p. 9.

9. Svendsen, *Milton and Science*, p. 48.

10. Arnold Williams, *The Common Expositor: An Account of the Commentaries on Genesis 1527–1633* (Chapel Hill: University of North Carolina Press, 1948), p. 43.

11. Milton, *The Christian Doctrine*, in *Complete Poems and Major Prose*, pp. 978–979.

12. Trophime Mourien, *The Creation*, trans. S.J. Tester, Twentieth Century Encyclopedia of Catholicism (New York: Hawthorne Books, 1962), p. 37.

13. Ladrière, *Language and Belief*, p. 179.

14. Dodd, *Parables of the Kingdom*, p. 16.

15. See Frederick Ferré's discussion of "The Logic of Analogy," *Language, Logic and God*, pp. 67–77.

16. Evans, *Language of Self-Involvement*, pp. 11–15.

17. Ibid., p. 223.

18. Ramsey, *Religious Language*, pp. 55–102.

19. Svendsen, *Milton and Science*, p. 233.

Chapter 7: Mammon, Models and Militancy

1. Herbert, "The Elixir," in *The Works of George Herbert*.

2. Owen Barfield, "Poetic Diction and Legal Fiction," *The Importance of Language*, ed. Max Black (Englewood Cliffs, N.J.: Spectrum Book, 1962), pp. 66–67.

3. Philip Wheelwright, *The Burning Fountain* (Bloomington: Indiana University Press, 1954), p. 17.

4. Burden, *The Logical Epic*, p. 1. My preference is for Anne Ferry's less rigid understanding of the verb "justify" in her counter-comment on I. 25–26: "To consider this opening statement in any way but as an organic poetic device, to extract it as a definitive and conclusive statement by Milton himself on the

meaning of this epic would be to conceive of *Paradise Lost* as if it were a theological treatise like *Of Christian Doctrine*. Milton intended his epic to answer a question or prove a proposition only in the ways that poetry can express meanings, ways entirely different from the abstract argumentations of his treatise." (Ferry, *Milton's Epic Voice*, pp. 8–9).

5. The characterization of the Enlightenment is Roger Shinn's ("The Holy," *A Handbook of Christian Theology* [Cleveland and New York: Meridian, 1958], p. 169).

6. Burden, *The Logical Epic*, p. 4.

7. Swardson, *Poetry and the Fountain of Light*, p. 146.

8. Auerbach, *Mimesis*, p. 14.

9. Swardson, *Poetry and the Fountain of Light*, p. 108.

10. Ibid., pp. 110–111.

11. *The Sermons of John Donne*, sermon 5, lines 14–47.

12. Swardson, *Poetry and the Fountain of Light*, p. 147.

13. I borrow the distinction between "picture" and "disclosure" models from Ian Ramsey. He likens "picture" models to similes in that they share "a descriptive use in respect of some important and relevant feature of the object the model." "Disclosure" models are like metaphors because they "generate a disclosure," yield "many possibilities of articulation," are not descriptive, and do not invite explanation or paraphrase. See Ian Ramsey, *Models and Mystery* (London and New York: Oxford University Press, 1964), pp. 48ff.

14. Swardson, *Poetry and the Fountain of Light*, p. 152.

15. The distinction I intend between parable and allegory is suggested by Robert Funk: "The parable does not lend itself to allegorization because parable as metaphor is designed to retain its own authority; the rationalization of its meaning tends to destroy its power as image . . . . The parable keeps the initiative in its own hand. Therein lies its hermeneutical potential." (Funk, *Language, Hermeneutic and the Word of God*, p. 152).

16. Ibid., p. 152.

17. Swardson, *Poetry and the Fountain of Light*, p. 147.

18. Ibid., pp. 113f.

19. Murray Roston, *Milton and the Baroque*, pp. 122–123.

20. Ibid., p. 124.

21. Quoted in Christopher Ricks' *Milton's Grand Style* (London, Oxford, New York: Oxford University Press, 1963), pp. 17–18.

22. Quoted in Roston, *Milton and the Baroque*, p. 116.

23. Quoted in James A. Freeman, *Milton and the Martial Muse: Paradise Lost and European Traditions of War* (Princeton: Princeton University Press, 1980), p. 13.

24. John Peter, *A Critique of Paradise Lost* (New York and London: Shoe String, 1960), p. 79.

25. Quoted in Roston, *Milton and the Baroque*, p. 116.

26. Freeman, *Milton and the Martial Muse*, p. 8.

27. Stein, *Answerable Style*, p. 20.

28. Roston, *Milton and the Baroque*, p. 118.

29. Ibid., p. 144.

30. Joseph Summers, *The Muse's Method* (New York: Norton, 1962), p. 129.

31. Summers, *Muse's Method*, pp. 136–137.

32. Fish, *Surprised by Sin*, p. 197.

33. Madsen, *From Shadowy Types to Truth*, pp. 110–111.

34. Ibid., p. 111n.

35. Ramsey, *Religious Language*, p. 179.

36. Ebeling, *Theological Theory of Language*, p. 192.

37. Baxter Hathaway, *Marvels and Commonplaces: Renaissance Literary Criticism* (New York: Random House, 1968), p. 144.

Chapter 8: *The Logic of Encounter*

1. Ebeling, *Theological Theory of Language*, p. 191.

2. Black, *Models and Metaphors*, p. 237.

3. Milton, *The Christian Doctrine*, in *Complete Poems and Major Prose*, p. 1012.

4. Basil Willey, *The Seventeenth Century Background: Studies on the Thought of the Age in Relation to Poetry and Religion* (New York: Columbia University Press, 1967), p. 255.

5. See Maurice Kelley, *This Great Argument* (Princeton: Princeton University Press, 1941), p. 149 n. 21; E.M.W. Tillyard, *Studies in Milton* (New York: Macmillan, 1951), p. 13; Millicent Bell, "The Fallacy of the Fall in *Paradise Lost*," *PMLA* 68 (1953), 874–875; A.J.A. Waldock, *Paradise Lost and Its Critics* (Cambridge: Cambridge University Press, 1964), pp. 222–223.

6. See, for example, J.M. Evans, *Paradise Lost and the Genesis Tradition* (Oxford: Oxford University Press, 1968), Chapter 10.

7. Tillyard, *Studies in Milton*, pp. 17–19.

8. Anthony Low, "The Parting in the Garden in *Paradise Lost*," *Philological Quarterly* 47 (1968), pp. 30–35.

9. John Peter, *Critique of Paradise Lost*, p. 118.

10. Ibid., pp. 118–119.

11. Fredson Bowers, "Adam, Eve, and the Fall in *Paradise Lost*," *PMLA*, 84 (1969), p. 270.

12. Joan Bennett, " 'Go': Milton's Antinomianism and the Separation Scene in *Paradise Lost*, Book 9," *PMLA*, 98 (1983), p. 398.

13. Ibid., p. 389.

14. See C.S. Lewis, *A Preface to Paradise Lost* (New York: Oxford University Press, 1961), pp. 73–78.

15. Torrance, "Faith and Philosophy," p. 237.

16. I paraphrase Antony Flew, *New Essays*, p. 96.

17. See Torrance on "objectivity," in "Faith and Philosophy," p. 237.

18. See Willey, *The Seventeenth Century Background*, p. 245.

19. Ibid., p. 29.

Selected Bibliography

Religious Language Studies

Auerbach, Erich. *Mimesis: the Representation of Reality in Western Literature.* tr. Willard Trask. Princeton: Princeton University Press, 1953.

Ayer, A.J.A. *Language, Truth and Logic.* 2nd. ed. New York: Dover Books, 1946.

Barfield, Owen. "Poetic Diction and Legal Fiction." In *The Importance of Language.* ed. Max Black. Englewood Cliffs, N.J.: Spectrum, 1962.

Bethune-Baker, J.F. *Introduction to the Early History of Christian Doctrine.* London: Methuen, n.d.

Bevan, Edwyn. *Symbolism and Belief: The Gifford Lectures 1933-1934.* London and Glasgow: Fontana, 1962.

Black, Max. *Models and Metaphors.* Ithaca, N.Y.: Cornell University Press, 1962.

Braithwaite, R.B. *An Empiricist's View of the Nature of Religious Belief.* Cambridge University Press, 1955.

Bultmann, Rudolph. *Jesus Christ and Mythology.* New York: Scribners, 1958.

_____. *Kerygma and Myth.* ed. H.W. Bartsch., tr. R.H. Fuller. New York: Harper Torchbook, 1961.

Burke, Kenneth. *The Rhetoric of Religion: Studies in Logology.* Berkeley, Los Angeles, London: University of California Press, 1970.

Cassirer, Ernst. *Language and Myth.* New York: Harper & Bros., 1946.

Cell, Edward. *Language Existence and God: Interpretations of Moore, Russell, Ayer, Wittgenstein, Wisdom, Oxford Philosophy and Tillich.* Nashville, Tenn.: and New York: Abingdon, 1971.

Crombie, I.M. *Faith and Logic.* London, 1958.

_____. "The Possibility of Theological Statements." *Religious Language and the Problem of Religious Knowledge.* ed. Ronald Santoni. Bloomington: Indiana University Press, 1968.

_____. "Theology and Falsification." *New Essays in Philosophical Theology.* ed. A.G.N. Flew and A. MacIntyre. London: SCM, 1955.

Crystal, David. *Linguistics, Language and Religion.* New York, 1965.

Crystal, David, and Derek Davy. *Investigating English Style.* English Language Series. gen. ed. Randolph Quirk. London: Longman's, 1969.

Dix, Dom Gregory. *The Shape of the Liturgy.* London, 1949.

Dodd, C.H. *The Parables of the Kingdom.* rev. ed. New York: Scribners, 1961.

Durrant, Michael. *The Logical Status of "God."* New Studies in Philosophy of Religion. gen. ed. W.D. Hudson. London and Basingstoke: Macmillan, 1973.

Ebeling, Gerhard. *Introduction to a Theological Theory of Language.* tr. R.A. Wilson. London: Collins, 1973.

Eliade, Mircea. *The Sacred and the Profane: the Nature of Religion.* tr. Willard R. Trask. New York and London: Harcourt Brace Jovanovich, 1959.

Evans, Donald. *The Logic of Self-Involvement: A Philosophical Study of Everyday Language with Special Reference to the Christian Use of Language about God as Creator.* London: SCM, 1963.

Farrar, A.M. *The Glass of Vision.* London: Dacre, 1948.

Ferré, Frederick. *Language, Logic and God.* New York, Evanston, London: Harper Torchbook, 1969.

Flew, Antony. "Philosophy and Language." *The Philosophical Quarterly* 5 (1955).

_____, and Alasdair MacIntyre, eds. *New Essays in Philosophical Theology.* London: SCM, 1955.

Funk, Robert. *Language, Hermeneutic and the Word of God.* New York: Harper & Row, 1966.

Haller, William. *The Rise of Puritanism.* New York: Harper Torchbook, 1957.

Hare, R.M. "Theology and Falsification." *New Essays in Philosophical Theology.* ed. A.G.N. Flew and A. MacIntyre. London: SCM, 1955.

Hartshorne, Charles. "The God of Religion and the God of Philosophy." *Talk of God,* Royal Institute of Philosophy Lectures. London and Basingstoke: Macmillan, 1969.

Hepburn, Ronald W. *Christianity and Paradox.* London: Watts, 1958.

Hick, John. *Faith and Knowledge.* Ithaca, N.Y.: Cornell University Press, 1957.

James, William. *The Varieties of Religious Experience.* London: Longman's Green, 1941.

Kaufmann, Walter. *Critique of Religion and Philosophy.* New York: Anchor, 1961.

Kleinknecht, H., J. Fichtner, G. Stahlin, et al. *Wrath.* tr. Dorothea M. Barton. ed. P.R. Ackroyd. Bible Key Words from Gerhard Kittel's *Theologisches Worterbuch zum Neuen Testament.* London: Adam & Charles Black, 1964.

Knappen, M.M. *Tudor Puritanism.* Chicago: University of Chicago Press, 1933.

Ladrière, Jean. *Language and Belief.* tr. Garrett Barden. Notre Dame: University of Notre Dame Press, 1972.

MacGregor, Geddes. *Aesthetic Experience in Religion.* London: Macmillan, 1947.

Macquarrie, John. *God-talk: An Examination of the Language and Logic of Theology.* London: SCM, 1967.

Martz, Louis. *The Poetry of Meditation.* rev. ed. New Haven, Conn.: Yale University Press, 1962.

Mascall, E. *Existence and Analogy.* London: Longman's, 1949.

_____. *Words and Images: a Study in Theological Discourse.* London: Libra, 1968.

Mitchell, Basil. "Theology and Falsification." *New Essays in Philosophical Theology.* London: SCM, 1955.

New, John F.H. *Anglican and Puritan: The Basis of their Opposition 1558–1604.* London: Adam and Charles Black, 1964.

Ogden, Schubert. *Christ Without Myth.* New York: Harper & Row, 1961.

Otto, Rudolf. *The Idea of the Holy.* tr. John W. Harvey. Harmondsworth: Penguin, 1923.

Palmer, Humphrey. *Analogy: A Study of Qualification and Argument in*

Theology. New Studies in Philosophy of Religion. gen ed. W.D. Hudson. London and Basingstoke: Macmillan, 1973.

Patrides, C.A. *"Paradise Lost* and the Language of Theology." *Language and Style in Milton*. ed. Ronald Emma and John Shawcross. New York: Ungar, 1967.

Petuchowski, Jakob J. *Theology and Poetry*. The Littman Library of Jewish Civilization. London, Henley and Boston: Routledge and Kegan Paul, 1978.

Phillips, D.Z. *The Concept of Prayer*. London: Routledge and Kegan Paul, 1965.

Ramsey, Ian T. *Models and Mystery*. London: Oxford University Press, 1964.

_____. *Religious Language: an Empirical Placing of Theological Phrases*. London: Victor Gollancz, 1946.

_____. *Words about God: the Philosophy of Religion*. London: SCM, 1971.

Robinson, N.H.G. "The Logic of Religious Language." *Talk of God*. Royal Institute of Philosophy Lectures. Volume II. London and Basingstoke: Macmillan, 1969.

Ross, Malcolm Mackenzie. *Poetry and Dogma*. New Brunswick: Rutgers University Press, 1954.

Russell, Bertrand. *Language and Reality*. London: George Allen & Unwin, 1939.

Ryle, Gilbert. "Systematically Misleading Expressions." In *Logic and Language (First Series)*. ed. A.G.N. Flew. Oxford: Basil Blackwell, 1955.

Santoni, Ronald, ed. *Religious Language and the Problem of Religious Knowledge*. Bloomington: Indiana University Press, 1968.

Smart, Ninian. "The Concept of Heaven." In *Talk of God*, Royal Institute of Philosophy Lectures. London and Basingstoke: Macmillan, 1969.

Stebbing, Susan. *A Modern Introduction to Logic*. 6th. ed. London: Methuen, 1948.

Torrance, T.F. "Faith and Philosophy." *Hibbert Journal*. XLVII (1949).

Underhill, Evelyn. *Mysticism: A Study in the Nature and Development of Man's Spiritual Consciousness*. 12th. ed. New York: Dutton, 1930.

Waismann, F. "Language Strata." In *Logic and Language (Second Series)*. ed. Antony Flew. Oxford: Basil Blackwell, 1955.

Wisdom, John. "Gods." In *Logic and Language (First Series)*. ed. Antony Flew. Oxford: Basil Blackwell, 1955.

Wheelwright, Philip. *The Burning Fountain: A Study in the Language of Symbolism*. rev. ed. Bloomington: Indiana University Press, 1968.

_____. *Metaphor and Reality*. Bloomington: Indiana University Press, 1962.

Willey, Basil. *The Seventeenth Century Background: Studies on the Thought of the Age in Relation to Poetry and Religion*. New York: Columbia University Press, 1967.

Wittgenstein, Ludwig. *Philosophical Investigations*. tr. G.E.M. Anscombe. Oxford: Basil Blackwell, 1953.

_____. *Tractatus Logico-Philosophicus*. tr. G.E.M. Anscombe. Oxford: Basil Blackwell, 1953.

Wood, Thomas. *English Casuistical Divinity during the Seventeenth Century*. London: SPCK, 1952.

Works on Literature, Milton and Paradise Lost

Bell, Millicent. "The Fallacy of the Fall in *Paradise Lost." PMLA* 68 (1953).

Bennett, Joan. " 'Go': Milton's Antinomianism and the Separation Scene in *Paradise Lost*, Book 9." *PMLA* 98 (1983).

Berek, Peter. " 'Plain' and 'Ornate' Styles and the Structure of *Paradise Lost. PMLA* LXXXV (March, 1970).

Berry, Boyd M. *Process of Speech: Puritan Religious Writing and* Paradise Lost. Baltimore: Johns Hopkins University Press, 1976.

Bowers, Fredson. "Adam, Eve, and the Fall in *Paradise Lost.*" PMLA 2 (March, 1969).

Broadbent, John B. *Some Graver Subject: An Essay on* Paradise Lost. New York: Barnes and Noble, 1960.

Burden, Dennis H. *The Logical Epic: A Study of the Argument of* Paradise Lost. Cambridge, Mass.: Harvard University Press, 1967.

Chatman, Seymour. "Milton's Participial Style." *PMLA* 83 (October, 1968).

Cope, Jackson I. *The Metaphorical Structure of* Paradise Lost. Baltimore: Johns Hopkins University Press, 1962.

Corcoran, [Sr.] Mary Irma. *Milton's* Paradise Lost *with Reference of the Hexameral Background.* Washington: Catholic University of America Press, 1945.

Curry, Walter Clyde. *Milton's Ontology, Cosmogony and Physics.* Lexington: University of Kentucky Press, 1957.

Emma, Ronald, and John Shawcross, eds. *Language and Style in Milton.* New York: Ungar, 1967.

Empson, William. *Milton's God.* rev ed. London: Chatto and Windus, 1965.

Evans, John M. Paradise Lost *and the Genesis Tradition.* Oxford: Clarendon Press, 1968.

Ferry, Anne Davidson. *Milton's Epic Voice: The Narrator in* Paradise Lost. Cambridge, Mass.: Harvard University Press, 1963.

Fish, Stanley. *Self-Consuming Artifacts: The Experience of Seventeenth-Century Literature.* Berkeley: University of California Press, 1972.

_____. *Surprised by Sin: The Reader in* Paradise Lost. London and New York: St. Martin's, 1967.

Freeman, James A. *Milton and the Martial Muse:* Paradise Lost *and the European Traditions of War.* Princeton, N.J.: Princeton University Press, 1980.

Frye, Roland Muschat. *God, Man and Satan: Patterns of Christian Thought and Life in* Paradise Lost, Paradise Regained *and the Great Theologians.* Princeton, N.J.: Princeton University Press, 1960.

_____. *Milton's Imagery and the Visual Arts: Iconographic Tradition in the Epic Poems.* Princeton, N.J.: Princeton University Press, 1978.

Gardner, Helen L. *A Reading of* Paradise Lost. Oxford: Clarendon Press, 1965.

Halewood, William. *The Poetry of Grace: Reformation Themes and Structures in English Seventeenth-Century Poetry.* New Haven, Conn.: Yale University Press, 1970.

Hathaway, Baxter. *Marvels and Commonplaces: Renaissance Literary Criticism.* New York: Random House, 1968.

Kelley, Maurice. *This Great Argument: A Study of Milton's de Doctrina Christiana as a Gloss upon* Paradise Lost. Gloucester, Mass.: Peter Smith, 1962.

Kerrigan, William. *The Prophetic Milton.* Charlottesville: University of Virginia Press, 1974.

_____. *The Sacred Complex.* Cambridge, Mass.: Harvard University Press, 1983.

Lewis, C.S. *A Preface to* Paradise Lost. New York: Oxford University Press, 1961.

Lieb, Michael. *The Dialectics of Creation: Patterns of Birth and Regeneration in* Paradise Lost. Amherst: University of Massachusetts Press, 1970.

MacCaffrey, Isabel. Paradise Lost *as "Myth."* Cambridge, Mass.: Harvard University Press, 1959.

Madsen, William G. *From Shadowy Types to Truth: Studies in Milton's Symbolism.* New Haven, Conn., and London: Yale University Press, 1968.

Martz, Louis. *The Paradise Within.* New Haven, Conn.: Yale University Press, 1964.

Merrill, Thomas F. *Christian Criticism: A Study of Literary God-Talk.* Amsterdam: Editions Rodopi, 1976.

Nuttall, Anthony David. *Overheard by God: Fiction and Prayer in Herbert, Milton, Dante and St. John.* London and New York: Methuen, 1980.

Patrides, C.A. *Milton and the Christian Tradition.* Oxford: Clarendon Press, 1966.

_____. "Paradise Lost and Language of Theology." In *Language and Style in Milton.* ed. Ronald Emma and John T. Shawcross. New York: Ungar, 1967.

Peter, John. *A Critique of* Paradise Lost. New York and London, 1960.

Rajan, B. Paradise Lost *and the Seventeenth Century Reader.* New York: Barnes and Noble, 1947.

Revard, Stella. *The War in Heaven:* Paradise Lost *and the Tradition of Satan's Rebellion.* Ithaca, N.Y.: Cornell University Press, 1980.

Ricks, Christopher. *Milton's Grand Style.* Oxford: Clarendon, 1963.

Riggs, William A. *The Christian Poet in* Paradise Lost. Berkeley: University of California Press, 1972.

Roston, Murray. *Milton and the Baroque.* Pittsburgh, Pa.: University of Pittsburgh Press, 1980.

Ryken, Leland. *The Apocalyptic Vision in Paradise Lost.* Ithaca, N.Y.: Cornell University Press, 1970.

Shawcross, John, and Ronald Emma, eds. *Language and Style in Milton.* New York: Ungar, 1967.

Sims, James. *The Bible in Milton's Epics.* Gainesville: University of Florida Press, 1962.

Stein, Arnold. *Answerable Style.* Minneapolis: University of Minnesota Press, 1953.

Summers, Joseph. *The Muse's Method.* Cambridge, Mass.: Harvard University Press, 1962.

Svendsen, Kester. *Milton and Science.* Cambridge, Mass.: Harvard University Press, 1956.

Swardson, H.R. *Poetry and the Fountain of Light.* London: George Allen & Unwin, 1962.

Sypher, Wylie. *Four Stages of Renaissance Style: Transformations in Art and Literature 1400–1700.* New York: Anchor, 1955.

Tayler, Edward W. *Milton's Poetry: Its Development in Time.* Pittsburgh, Pa.: Duquesne University Press, 1978.

Waldock, A.J.A. *Paradise Lost and Its Critics.* Cambridge: Cambridge University Press, 1947.

Willey, Basil. *The Seventeenth Century Background: Studies in the Thought of the Age in Relation to Poetry and Religion.* New York: Columbia University Press, 1967.

Williams, Arnold. *The Common Expositor: An Account of the Commentaries on Genesis 1527–1633.* Chapel Hill: University of North Carolina Press, 1948.

Wittreich, Joseph A. *Visionary Poetics: Milton's Tradition and His Legacy.* San Marino, Calif.: Huntington Library, 1979.

Index